Foreword by Les Brown

YOU ARE ENOUGH

Presented By Dr. Cheryl Wood

ISBN: 978-1-7923-6845-5
Kindle ISBN: 978-1-7923-6846-2

You Are Enough

FOREWORD... 9

    Les Brown

INTRODUCTION 11

    Dr. Cheryl Wood

You Are Enough To THRIVE In Corporate America........................ 15

    Lisa D. Anderson

Reclaim Your Power 19

    Diann Antley

From Doubting to Dominating 23

    David Banks, Ph.D.

Walk In Your Purpose 27

    Patricia Barnes

Your Pain Has a Purpose 31

    Stephanie Barnes

Enough Said.. 35

    Debra Bell-Campbell

Run *Your* Race... 39

    Tamika L. Blythers

Move Over. There Is Room At The Top For All.............................. 43

    Olenthia R. Boardley

It's All About Believing 47

    Audrey A. Boudreaux

You Are Enough to... Leave Your Legacy! 51

    Martina Britt Yelverton

Paid & Free... 55

Latasha Brooks

Dear "D.I.V.A" You Are Enough..................................... 59

Serena Brothers-Mohamed

Overcoming the Storms.. 63

Dr. Trina D. Brown

Cultivate Your Greatness 67

Linda Caldwell-Boykin

Dating My Husband Again.. 71

Leona Carter

Ready or Not, Take your Shot... 75

Dr. Elizabeth A. Carter

I am BRANDED BY GOD™ and So Are YOU!................ 79

Kim Carter Evans

Set Your Reminder. God Is Ready To Put You On-Demand! 83

Avis Cherie'

It's Time To Walk In Your Gifts....................................... 87

Kearn Crockett Cherry

You Are Enough To Profit From Your Purple 91

Joyce Chesley Hayward

Born To Shine! 95

Judie Clark

Don't Shrink Back.. 99

Tesha D. Colston

You Are Enough To Break The Cycle Of Generational Poverty!.... 103

JJ Conway

You Are Enough for A Bomb Relationship 107

    Montrella S. Cowan, MSW, LICSW

Trust God's Divine Timing 111

    Lisa J. Crawford

Queen, Shine Bright Like a Diamond 115

    Min. Nakita Davis

Become Your Own Boss 121

    Monique Denton-Davis

You Are Enough - To Overcome Adversity 125

    Dr. Toscha L. Dickerson

Believe It and You Can Achieve It! 129

    Patrina Dixon

You are Enough for Making Self-Care Essential 131

    Jacqueline R. Duncan

You Are Enough To Overcome The Unknown Zone! 135

    Dr. Monique Flemings

When Your Value Is Clear, Your Decision Is Easy! 139

    Dr. Jonas Gadson, DTM

You Really Are Enough! 143

    T. Renee Garner

Pain to Purpose 147

    Dr. Chere M. Goode

Your Vision is Your Victory 151

    Mijiza A. Green

You Are Enough To DOMINATE Your Emotional Currency! 155

    Brittany Greene

You Are Enough To Make It Matter! 159

    Ryan C. Greene

Message From Me-To-Me 163

    Christopher Hampton

Unlock Your Purpose: The World is Waiting on You! 167

    Rasheda Hatchett, MN, RN

Finding Beauty in Your Brokenness 171

    Andrea Hayden

No Warranty… As-Is 175

    Gene E. Hayden, Jr.

Faith the Size of a Mustard Seed 179

    Phyllis Lenora Henry

Created by the Creator to be Enough! 183

    Donna Hicks Izzard

Pivot, Prepare And Lead With Confidence 187

    Dr. Karen Hills Pruden

Your Shine is Enough 191

    B. Jacqueline Jeter

You Are Enough to Thrive After 40 195

    Ingrid Lamour-Thomas

You Are Enough To Take Your Financial Power Back 199

    Erica Lane

You Are Enough To Attack And Overcome Your Distractions 203

    Saymendy Lloyd

You Are the Apple of God's Eye 207

    Dr. Nicole S. Mason

You Can Do It 211
    Jocelin T. McElderry, RN, BSN

Overcome Fear – Achieve Your Purpose 213
    Dr. Theresa A. Moseley

Know Your Worth. NO Apologies.. 217
    Carol T. Muleta

Triumph Over Trauma.. 221
    Emma Norfleet-Haley

The Magic Pen... 225
    Ene Obi

Your Story Makes Heroes 229
    Suzanne Peters

Keep Your Temple Healthy, Stop Filling It With C.R.A.P.!............. 233
    Tanya Y. Pritchett, PMP

You Are Enough as God Intended…... 237
    Debbie T. Proctor-Caldwell

Self-Care Is Not A Beauty Regimen 241
    Tykesha Reed

Right to Thrive 245
    Nikki Rogers

You Are Enough to be Broken and Beautiful.................................... 249
    Jacqueline Shaulis

You Are Enough to Live a Purposeful Life.................................... 253
    Dr. Onika L. Shirley

You Are Enough to Build Your Empire 257
    Dr. Carlisa M. Smith

Walk in Confidence 261

    CoWano Ms Coco Stanley

Disappointment to Purpose.. 265

    Angelecia Stewart

You are Enough to Fulfill the Promises God has Spoken 269

    Teara F. Stewart

Wake Up; You Are Unstoppable! 273

    Dr. Carmen Thomas

Your Greenhouse of Greatness... 277

    Michelle S. Thomas

Grace for The Finish Line 281

    Simene' Walden

Let Your Soul Radiate 285

    Stephanie Wall

You Are Enough to Carry Your Vision... 289

    Dr. Saundra Wall Williams

You Are Enough to S.L.A.Y. Your Finances 293

    Dr. Ranelli A. Williams, CPA

Own Your Power: It's Your Fearless Force Within 297

    Carolyn Wilson

You Are Right! 301

    Darius "The Professor" Wise

Winning in Life at Your Pace.. 305

    Dr. Debra Wright Owens

FOREWORD

By Les Brown

You have something special, you have GREATNESS in YOU!

If you have followed my career or heard me speak, then you know that I believe that all of us were born with a purpose and that we all have great gifts inside just waiting to come out and be shared with the world.

As much as I know this to be true, I can't tell you how many people I've met or who send me messages asking me to help them tap into or discover this greatness that I mention so often.

These people are a lot like I was many years ago, they are suffering from what I call, possibility blindness. They can't see the possibilities, potential, and promise that life holds for them. I understand how that feels. They feel like it's possible for others, but feel that they either aren't worthy or don't have enough money, skills, or resources to change the direction of their lives and achieve success.

Have you ever felt this way? I did for quite a long time, until I finally discovered that I was ENOUGH!

Guess what... You are Enough too!

YOU ARE ENOUGH

I am excited to share with you Dr. Cheryl Wood's latest groundbreaking book, You are Enough.

We all need a little coaching from time to time to help us walk into and or remain focused on our internal greatness and I'm glad that Cheryl is here to provide us with this gem. Prepare to uncover and overcome the mental and emotional barriers in your life that are blocking you from receiving the blessings and gifts that you deserve.

Dr. Wood shares with us that no matter what seems to be broken, imperfect, or flawed in you, that you can still win because despite your circumstances, You are Enough!

There is no one in this world quite like you and we need what you have to offer.

I hope you're ready to transform your mind and your life, because reading these pages will certainly push you forward and accelerate your journey into greatness.

I keep this book close by me to feel inspired and motivated. I'm sure you will too!

Remember You are Enough!

That's my story and I'm sticking to it.

Les Brown
Speaker, Author, Trainer

INTRODUCTION

By Dr. Cheryl Wood

Compilation Visionary of You Are Enough
14x Best-Selling Author | International Empowerment Speaker |
TEDx Speaker | Speaker Development Coach | Leadership Expert

You Are Enough just as you are! You are an irreplaceable expression of life, a one-of-a-kind precious masterpiece, the likes of which no one will ever see again. You are powerful beyond all measure. And you have everything you need to win BIG in life… in fact, winning is in your DNA! But you must believe it before anyone else will believe it.

From this moment forward, regardless of your fears, doubts or self-limiting beliefs, I challenge you to boldly embrace ownership of the proclamation that You Are Enough. You are uniquely designed and made to be exactly who you are on purpose, with purpose, and for a purpose. You are enough as you are, flaws and all, beautiful and broken. You never have to strive to become more worthy, more valid, or more accepted. It is no mistake that you are this person, in this place, at this time. Because you are unique, no one else can fulfill your divine purpose, therefore, the world needs you to show-up in all of your God-given greatness without excuses. You have everything it takes to become who you want to be and live the life you want to live.

In this book, you will be reminded that becoming the best version of yourself will require ongoing courage, tenacity, drive, ambition, determination and commitment. On your life's journey, you will face challenges, obstacles, roadblocks and setbacks but your internal strength will equip you to bounce back from anything standing in the way of your destiny. You are enough to develop the mental toughness necessary to propel yourself forward and to soar beyond all limitations. Don't forget to remind yourself of who you are and whose you are on a daily basis!

As you immerse yourself into each of the personal messages contained in this book, it is my hope that you will recall to mind that you are destined for greatness and that you owe it to yourself to step out into the deep to explore what is possible for your life. You Are Enough will reignite a fire within you to use your unique fingerprint to create a life you're in love with and to make a difference in the lives of others who will be inspired by your life journey.

In my own life, I had to go on a personal journey of discovering that I was enough regardless of my past. As a young girl who was raised in poverty in an inner-city housing project in Baltimore, Maryland, I assumed that my life would be dictated by my environment. I assumed that people would judge who I could be based on where I had come from, and that I would be just another statistic like many of the other youth in my neighborhood. But there was a turning point when I started to shift my mindset and my perspective in order to make a decision that I didn't want to be a statistic. I wanted to rise above my past and become a change agent in the world who would impact the lives of men and women globally! Once I made the decision to do more, become more and walk fully in my divine purpose, I allowed my actions to prove my intentions.

As I have continued to acknowledge that I am enough just as I am, it has positioned me to become more confident, driven, determined and tenacious in sharing my voice, using my gifts, and making my mark in the world instead of simply staying quiet and accepting whatever life hands me. I have become more aware, confident and conscious of the need to play all out in life for as long as I have breath in my body. I have become a willing vessel to equip, empower and inspire women globally to develop new levels of confidence in their own lives and to come to the front of the room to share their voice and their gifts. After all, our lives should always be bigger than ourselves. And that's the belief system that each co-author in this book holds strongly – that their life is bigger than themselves and that their greatest impact in the world will always stem from sharing their authentic stories, experiences, and expertise to inspire and empower others.

As you take a deep dive into the messages shared in You Are Enough, it is my hope that you will feel enlightened, reenergized and reignited for the impact and legacy you are meant to create in the world. It is my deep hope that you will be reminded of your own strength and that you will dream a little bigger, fight a little harder for what you want, bounce back a little quicker when you get knocked down, and never ever give up. You were not created to be ordinary, you were designed to be EXTRAordinary!

I celebrate each of the co-authors of the You Are Enough book project for selflessly sharing their messages of inspiration and empowerment. Each message will propel you to develop a new mindset, attitude, behaviors and patterns in order to live your best lie. As you immerse yourself in the You Are Enough book, you will be reminded that you matter and the world needs you to know You Are Enough so you can fulfill your destiny and your soul purpose.

Dr. Cheryl Wood
Compilation Visionary of You Are Enough
WEBSITE: www.cherylempowers.com
EMAIL: info@cherylwoodempowers.com
SOCIAL MEDIA: @CherylEmpowers

YOU ARE ENOUGH

You Are Enough To THRIVE In Corporate America

By Lisa D. Anderson

*"Authenticity is the daily practice of letting go of who
we think we're supposed to be and embracing who we
are."*
Brené Brown

You are enough to thrive (not just survive) in Corporate America. I use the term "Corporate America" loosely; you are enough to thrive (not just survive) in your workplace. The institution of Corporate America has its own ideals of the way you should act, behave, look, and conform in order for you to be successful. In addition, every workplace has its own culture, rules, and unwritten rules on how to navigate the environment. For a woman of color, this can lead to not feeling confident, feelings of being invisible, and the lack of courage for showing up as your true authentic self. The "mask" goes on.

I know the feeling of wearing that mask. As I was growing my career in Human Resources, the higher I stepped on the career ladder, I started to add layers to the mask to the point that I was starting to become a different person. A person that wasn't me, a person that I didn't like. As I had different experiences in my career, I started to second guess myself, and my voice started to disappear. I allowed other people's opinions about me to impact the way I "showed up." It started to have a negative impact on me, personally.

[15]

YOU ARE ENOUGH

If you have experienced this or are currently experiencing this in your career, you are not alone. It can feel lonely because you may not have a support system or someone you can lean on (or trust) to share what you're experiencing. There are others that feel the same way, but they also have their mask on (and their guard up), so it continues to feel lonely.

The good news is that there are strategies for removing the mask so that you can show up as your true authentic self. You are enough. There is no mistake. You were put in that position, in that organization, in that workplace for a reason. It's time for you to step into your power, and that means the power of YOU, no one else, YOU.

A key strategy for removing the mask is to get back to basics and honor your values. Through my experience, I learned that the mask went on when I started to NOT honor my values. When you're not honoring your values, things become very uncomfortable for you. Go back to the basics, get clear on your values, and honor them. If your values do not align with the organization's values, it's time to assess whether you should be working there.

You are enough to thrive (not just survive) in Corporate America. Be proud of the person you are. We are all unique, and there's a place for you in Corporate America. If you're working in a place that doesn't appreciate YOU and what you bring to the table (your uniqueness and brilliance), find another workplace. Find a workplace culture that will embrace you for who you are. Fearfully and Wonderfully Made (Psalms 139:14).

BIO:

Lisa Anderson is the President of Positively in Pursuit. She is a certified Leadership Coach who has 25 years of HR experience. She focuses on women in leadership on finding their leadership voice, building their leadership courage, and increasing their executive presence to propel their careers.

Lisa still works full-time in Corporate America as a Chief HR Officer (CHRO). She has worked at every level of HR growing her career from a Recruiter to Chief HR Officer (CHRO). She works with her clients on next-level career success, leadership branding, and strategic career positioning.

YOU ARE ENOUGH

Reclaim Your Power
By Diann Antley

"A person's steps are directed by the Lord. How then can anyone understand their own way?"
Proverbs 20:24 NIV

Royal One,

I want to let you know that there's power in your pivot. From divorce, from bankruptcies, from any life occurrence that has caused you to pause. You may have tried new things several times and failed. You may not understand why you should move, so you've chosen to remain still. That stillness caused stagnation and confusion, which resulted in you feeling powerless. It is not too late for you to take your power back!

The power will come from forgiving and releasing.

Forgive those who have wronged you. Chances are while you are still thinking about that person, they are living life without giving you a second thought. Take your power back. Forgive them, then forgive yourself for how you may have reacted and responded. Pivot.

This reminds me of when I was going through my divorce. One Sunday I was at my church's parking lot, when I heard my "inner voice" tell me to call my WASband and ask for forgiveness. Initially, I

[19]

didn't understand why I was the one to reach out, so I was hesitant with communicating. But I trusted God more than my lack of understanding. When I hung up the phone, I felt a sense of release. I no longer had to be angry or resentful, so I let those feelings go. Once I did, I was able to pivot and begin my journey of reclaiming my power.

You have been given the power for a purpose. Pivot and take your power back.

Release those emotions that no longer serve you. Holding on to anger, resentment, and shame while continuously experiencing each one is unhealthy. It is time for you to pivot, get off that Emotional Raceway, and free your mind from the negative thinking. Once you do, your mind will be free to pivot towards a more empowered state. Release, so you can receive.

When you forgive and release, you will be able to pivot into the life you were meant to live. That life is filled with all the yummy-goodness God has waiting for you.

Queens and Kings, your powerful place is waiting.

Pivot, and reclaim your power.

BIO:

Diann Antley is a Forgiveness Coach with Anew You, Clarified LLC, a Coaching and Consulting Firm designed to help Divorced, Christians to forgive & release, so that they can reclaim their power and embrace their purpose. Diann is also a Speaker, Author, Internet Show Host, and Radio/TV Co-Host. Diann understands the journey and realizes the importance of telling her story to inspire others and help them reclaim their power & embrace their purpose.

To learn more about Diann, website her at www.anewyouclarified.com

Connect with Diann socially on these platforms!

FB: https://www.facebook.com/diann.antley

@diannantleyspeaks

IG: @iamdiannantley

LI: https://www.linkedin.com/in/diann-antley/

YOU ARE ENOUGH

From Doubting to Dominating
By David Banks, PhD

*" ... because He who is in you is greater than he who
is in the world."*
1 John 4:4b

Do you know that what is *in* you is more powerful than what is around you, what is behind you, and whatever hinders you from moving forward?

When I was in the seventh grade, I worked up the courage to try out for the varsity basketball team. Towering at over six feet, I was confident I would be an asset to our small-town team. On the day of the tryouts, I suited up ready to show the coach my skills. After tryouts, I showered and ran to see if I made the team. I started at the top of the list, and there it was, David Banks. I could hardly catch my breath. I couldn't wait to go home and share this exciting news with my dad.

My dad was a big and tall man. He was a serious man and focused on providing for the family. And my mom was the encourager and motivator of the family. By the time I got home, Dad was sitting in his favorite chair, dozing in and out of sleep from a long day at work.

I walked toward him with a big grin on my face and said, "Hey Dad, guess what? I made the varsity basketball team."

YOU ARE ENOUGH

I thought he would give me a fist bump and dream with me that I would be the next Magic Johnson or Dr. J.

He opened his eyes and stared into my eyes, and said, "Boy, you know you are not going to succeed at basketball, and you will never go to the NBA."

After those frigid words, he closed his eyes and went back to sleep. That experience with my dad left me empty and full of questions. Am I good enough? Will I ever succeed at anything? Will anybody believe in me? These questions led me on a search. I made it my mission to discover the answers to these questions. My turning point came from this book I read, *In Pursuit of Purpose*, by Dr. Myles Munroe. After reading the book, I realized the answers to these questions were not around me but inside me. This revelation is the fundamental principle that I use in every facet of my life.

I understood I am designed for my purpose, which was established before I was born. My purpose is my *why* and supersedes my past and anyone's opinion of me.

After I discovered and embraced my purpose, I went from doubting to dominating. I transitioned from asking, "AM I?" to declaring, "I AM A SUCCESS! I AM ENOUGH!"

This is my charge to each of you. Be brave, confront your doubts about yourself. Be mindful that what's inside you is greater than those doubts. What you have been through does not define you. You are designed for greatness. Take hold of this principle and move from doubting to dominating in your BEST LIFE!

BIO:

Dr. David Banks is president of Noble Success Strategic Group. He is a certified speaker, certified professional trainer, and a wholeness coach and author.

As a professional coach, he specializes in relationship development, success development, leadership development, and motivation, and purpose discovery.

Dr. Banks speaks to government leaders, ministry leaders and corporate leaders. He is a global speaker who empowers people to discover their inner greatness to conquer their doubts, so they can dominate in their life.

Dr. David Banks and his lovely bride, Lady Sylvia, reside in Chattanooga, TN with their three children. Please check out my website: www.drdavidLbanks.com to learn more.

YOU ARE ENOUGH

Walk In Your Purpose
By Patricia Barnes

"Blessed is she who has believed that the Lord would
fulfill His promises to her!"
Luke 1:45

When she believed ...

She started to crawl, then walk. Now she is running and thriving in her purpose because she relied on the Lord more than herself. God said, "you're enough to start the business, write the book, dream bigger, walk in your purpose, and have healthy relationships. You can have it all despite how you were raised, your background, your past, limited resources, and minimum help. Nothing has come easy for you, and you haven't had the luxury of handouts."

I'm here to affirm with you. Repeat these declarations:

I AM ENOUGH!

I AM MORE THAN ENOUGH!

I AM WORTHY!

I AM DESTINED FOR GREATNESS!

VICTORY BELONGS TO ME!

YOU ARE ENOUGH

I'M COMING FOR IT!

Start where you are with what you have! Let go of perfectionism! Learn as you go! You don't have to have it all figured out. I promise God will work out the details with each step you take. Be willing to do the work and never give up, regardless of your fears, insecurities, whether it's been done before or if you don't feel ready. Forget about the negative things people who don't believe in you say! Believe in yourself! When you can't believe in yourself, read the scripture Luke 1:45 until you believe it. Write it down! Post it on your refrigerator! Frame it on the wall - anywhere you can consistently read it! Affirm and shout: "It's my time. I won't stop until I get everything God promised me!!!"

How to discover your purpose

Your purpose is the reason you were born. Purpose inspires you to make the world a better place. Think of the things you're great at that take minimal effort. What gets you excited? What makes you mad? What is something you wouldn't mind doing for free, and people often compliment you on?

Prayer for purpose

"God, light the fire that dwells within us as we walk boldly in purpose. Grant us the audacity and authority to know we are enough! We pray for perseverance to overcome obstacles trying to prevent us from receiving all the promises You have prepared for us! May each obstacle be a reminder that victory can only be achieved when we fight through the rough path. May every plot attempting to destroy us guide us to the next level. When we feel anxious, remind us to pray and worry about nothing. Send people who can help us build the vision and uplift us when we want to quit. May it forever be imprinted in our heart and mind to propel us towards greatness that 'with man this is impossible, but with God all things are possible.'"

Read my story about how God will use your pain, flaws, fears, struggles, insecurities, trials, and tribulations for purpose and turn it into power and triumph. Read the blog, Purpose for Pain and Motivated by Fear at gopatty.com. Listen to the Custom Life podcast hosted by Kadisha White on all podcast platforms, Episode 5, "The Purpose-Filled Life."

BIO:

Patricia Barnes is a registered nurse, blogger, motivational speaker, #1 best-selling author, mentor, coach, and founder of Go Patty LLC. Go Patty is a movement to inspire, motivate, and empower others to overcome pain, fears, and insecurities and become whole spiritually, personally, interpersonally, mentally, emotionally, and financially. Consistently work on personal development, dream big, then take action, and always have fun along the way.

Website and blog - gopatty.com

Facebook and Instagram- @gopattybrand

Email - gopattybrand@gmail.com

YOU ARE ENOUGH

Your Pain Has a Purpose
By Stephanie Barnes

*"No one can duplicate who you are, so why not
Maximize Your Unique Identity!"*
Stephanie Barnes

Do you ever notice when you're in the grocery store how challenging it can be to choose an item that basically serves the same purpose? For example, my favorite salad dressing is Catalina [French], which comes in three options: Original, Lite, and Fat-Free, and based on what stage I'm at in my life at the time, that helps me to determine which one I'll choose.

Let's go a little deeper. We're going to do some flip-flopping, but in the end, you should get the picture. I'm a Survivor of Domestic Abuse as well as a Recovering Drug Addict, and as a result, I was arrested for a crime and sentenced to 10 - 15 years. I mean, it was one of the most excruciating, scariest, and embarrassing pains that I had to endure. The way the system works, when you arrive at the police station, you go through the "Intake" process. After obtaining your demographic information, the officer takes your mugshot, gets your fingerprints, verifies if you have any tattoos or markings on your body, and assigns you a unique number. Based on that number, you now have a new man-made identity.

Now, envision yourself in the theme of the salad dressing. Regardless of which brand we choose as the consumers, they all have their unique ingredients for the purpose it serves. If they had feared putting their brand out there because of similar products or, should I say, similar identities of their competitors, they would've never known the outcome of their success and accomplishments. The same applies to you. Someone out there will benefit from your unique identity as you become their favorite or relatable choice, but you can't become their choice until you decide that You Are Enough to step out of your doubts, fears, and limiting beliefs.

If I would've settled with the mindset and concept of not being enough because of a man-made identification system [which currently has me categorized with a felony record], I'd be cheating myself out of personally experiencing God's Purpose for my Pain. I love what I do, as to why I get up daily and fight not only for myself but for others that share relatable personal experiences and pain. You see, most of life's pain comes from having your unseasoned desires met, and when your Pain Has a Purpose, you have to make up your mind and trust the self-developing process as you "Become The Who In You." For that person, thing, and situation that caused my pain, God showed me that I have the Power to maximize what's in my hands. My hands have a unique identity to create anything I push to have, and with such a greater calling on my life, I know that I'm someone's answer. So, I refuse to settle based on a man-made identification system.

Regardless of the mess, distress, pain, and regrets you've encountered, there's only "One You," and God did not duplicate another. You Are Enough, and Your Pain Has a Purpose ~ Genesis 1:27.

BIO:

As a Washington, D.C. native, victim, and advocate of Domestic and Drug Abuse, my voice is used to inspire women. As Co-Author of Pray, Pursue, Persist, and Women Crushing Mediocrity, I have an insatiable appetite to connect with audiences of diverse backgrounds to maximize their potential. Spending time with God is a priority; cross-country traveling is my mental reset, and vibing to music soothes my soul.

Dedications: Rosa Barnes (Mother), Samuel Armstrong (Father), Maehalie Barnes (92 Years Young Nana), Delma Parks (Aunt, Spiritual Advisor), and a host of family and friends.

Contact:

Website: www.globalvisionprod.com

YouTube: Global Vision Productions

Facebook & Instagram: @globalvisionprod

Email: globalvisionprod@gmail.com

YOU ARE ENOUGH

Enough Said

By Debra Bell-Campbell

*"Life is a fight for territory and once you stop fighting
for what you want, what you don't want will
automatically take over."*
Les Brown

Who are you? I am Noah and Mary's daughter, the eighth of twelve
siblings, Eddie Xavier's mom, CEO of Inspired Visions Consulting
Group, LLC, Director of Staff Development & Training, international
speaker, author, coach, and wellness strategist. I am the remnants of
my ancestors. As exciting as these titles may be, the hunt to find me
still exists. Allow me to challenge **you** to rediscover who you truly are.

How much time have you spent waiting for someone to validate you,
obtain one more certification, one more pat on the back, or permission
to prove that you are worthy? The stench of doubt surrounds you like a
spoiled egg. When will you draw the line and fight for yourself? The
fight is within you and has always been. Recognizing it requires you to
peel back the layers of who others have proclaimed you to be. This
necessitates the deepest level of introspection. No one said the fight
would be easy or fair. In fact, according to David Hackworth, "if you
find yourself in a fair fight, you did not plan your mission properly."

Circumstances and events shape us as we are hit hard with the reality
of the choices we make. While juggling all those titles, I had no
control over my circumstances that led me on the hunt to find myself.

[35]

YOU ARE ENOUGH

Death is a profound event and often leaves us feeling depleted and lost. My parent's (particularly my dad) passing within eight months of each other was the catalyst that ignited my quest to truly accept me. August 7, 2015, was the day my daddy died. Suddenly, I sprang to my feet as I heard my sister Carol's chilling scream. I ran into the living room, where I saw my dad slumped in his favorite rocking chair. There, I performed CPR on my dad until the Paramedics arrived. I performed cycles of 30 compressions and two breaths. As I attempted to breathe life into him, it was at that moment I felt the urgency to resuscitate my own life. Moreover, I realized that I could not hide anymore. I was the first one to experience my father's last breath. This was the first time in my life I felt as if I showed up when it mattered the most. I emerged visible, self-assured, and aware that all I needed to impact the world was within me. I was enough!

In conclusion, the fight to show up as authentically you is based on your ability to make the **S.H.I.F.T (Stop Hiding Inside and Face Your Truth).** Here are two strategies you can use to give you a fighting chance to always show up as uniquely you:

- **Affirm and Believe in yourself:** Assertively remind yourself of who you are!

- **Never give up:** Success is the culmination of daily small steps.

Ready to **S.H.I.F.T**? Contact me @ debrabell-campbell.com.

BIO:

As one of the most sought-after introverted women leadership experts, Debra Bell-Campbell is an MBTI Certified Practitioner, National Certified Counselor, Wellness Coach, author, and dynamic speaker. With over 15 years of coaching women in leadership in private and corporate settings, she has designed, developed, and delivered exceptional programs to promote and enhance professional and personal growth. She is passionate about helping her clients revel in their success in a "true to you" nature, reminding clients to embrace the mind and body connection. Ultimately, every client must **S.H.I.F.T**- (**S**top **H**iding **I**nside, & **F**ace **Y**our **T**ruth).

YOU ARE ENOUGH

Run *Your* Race

By Tamika L. Blythers

"The Race Is Not To The Swift Or Strong, But To
Those Who Endure To The End."
Ecclesiastes 9:11

Why are we so obsessed with reality shows? I guess it's just something about seeing or being on the chopping block facing elimination and humiliation. To hear, "you are the weakest link," "you have been chopped," "your journey ends today," or "you're just not ready" makes us want to stand around and watch the modern-day lynching. Clearly, society has fully accepted this judgmental, dysfunctional behavior as the "new normal." Why do we readily accept negative labels and false narratives about ourselves and our lives? We must start believing and positively increasing our own belief system. So, let's talk about this thing called "being enough." Who told you that you're not enough and what is the measuring stick used to say, "I am Enough"? How many likes, loves, degrees, certifications, and titles does it take for you to feel like you *are* enough? Most importantly, why did you buy into that harmful garbage anyway?

There are ordinary people out here doing magnificent things every single day. They do not have "superpower" blood, but they do have super strong faith and tenacity. Change your mind and your perspective will shift dramatically. The ones who have never tried it have the most to say.

YOU ARE ENOUGH

We've got to stop adopting everybody else's definition of "enough." Only you can grant people permission to make *you* feel inadequate. Who told you were naked? Whose report do you choose to believe?

I'm reminded of an old 70's movie about a young teenager babysitting and receiving strange phone calls in the middle of the night. The annoying calls were traced by the police and to her surprise, the terrifying calls were being made from within the home. Oftentimes, it's really not other people that are doing the most damage. It is "us," and the call is coming from within.... OUR OWN HOUSE!!! Abuse, abandonment, divorce, severe loss, and trauma are heavy, life-changing events. If left unaddressed, you will continue to receive negative calls from within. Your greatest competition is the mind. Stop comparing your first chapter to their fifteenth. Embrace your journey, enjoy the scenery.

Are you holding on to "good" when God is trying to bless you with "greater"? Why are we faithful to dead things and are they really that comfortable? By natural default, stagnation has major implications. In order to fully understand change, we must embrace three powerful truths: Change is difficult. Change is necessary for growth. Change is inevitable. When you go, you grow, and if you stay, you will decay. You will *always* rise to the level of your expectations.

Your life lesson for today is: You are the "locksmith" for your life, so change the keys...change your destiny!!! Three life tips I would like to share are:

- Focus on who *you* are.

- Value what *you* bring to the table.

- Master *your* craft and talents.

BIO:

Tamika L. Blythers is a master trainer and facilitator, author, educator, entrepreneur, consultant, and transformational speaker. Her platform, "V.O.W" 9 points of Impact, is a simple shared message of self-inquiry, which requires individuals to radically change perspectives about decisions and goals in life. Her consulting business, EduVizon, LLC, provides empowerment education and hosting/emcee services designed to enhance, energize, and provide clarity while transforming and achieving desired premium results. She has authored several books, two of which are best sellers.

She is the "Upperroom Writer."

T.L. Blythers stands firmly on the life principle, "You are a product of your expectations, not the limitations."

YOU ARE ENOUGH

Move Over. There Is Room At The Top For All

By Olenthia R. Boardley

"It always seems impossible until it's done."
Nelson Mandela

Imagine you are in your office grinding. Are you really grinding or just moving paper around? You have been thinking about this for a long time. Come on, fill out the application, attach the money, and press submit. Now you're grinding. You are grinding toward your own business. So, what if you are the 80th Speaker, Jeweler, Caterer, or Burger Truck owner? It doesn't matter. Your products and services you have to offer are the best of you, and no one can do you but you. So, go on do it!! Move over. There is room at the top for all. Remember, we have a global world to serve. We need your contributions. Stop being so selfish.

For years, I talked myself out of taking the steps to launch my business. So, yes, I fell short, bumped my head more than a few times, but found the courage to keep moving and trying. If I can do it, you can too. It does not have to be perfect. We learn as we grow. Connect yourself with people who are willing to mentor and support your growth. I was afraid to ask for help. I would say, "I got this," but I did not; I needed help. I felt I would be perceived as weak or, better yet, slow, something I have struggled with since elementary school. What I discovered is I can go at my own pace and still conquer. So, can you. Go on, put on your big girl or big boy underwear, take a deep breath,

[43]

and dive in. While swimming, look back for just a moment and give yourself a pat on the back for what you have accomplished. You are not being arrogant; it's okay to praise yourself. The truth is, you might be the only one giving yourself praise. Friends and family won't understand your passion. Don't let them get into your head. Don't let them slow you up or stop you. Put on your blinders and go full steam ahead. Find yourself a quiet place. Write down some business options you would like to develop.

Now the journey begins. Research tools you will need to start your business. Invest in a coach or classes to help and guide you. e You are now on your way. What a great feeling just to get started! Now, we have a new entrepreneur offering products and services to so many who need You. Remember these three things: 1. It's Your Drea; no one can take that from you. 2. Go for I; if you don't, you will always wonder, "I would have, I could have." 3. Dreams Do Come True, when you work hard, you will be truly amazed and surprised at what I know you can do. You Got This!! Move Over There is Room At The Top For All!

Contact me: https://www.orbsroyaltreatment.com/

https://www.instagram.com/orbsroyaltreatment/

OLENTHIA R. BOARDLEY

BIO:

Olenthia R. Boardley is an Event Designer and Chief Business Officer of Orbs Royal Treatment. Since 1997, Mrs. Boardley has produced and managed numerous business and wedding productions. Having a B.S. in Business and Information Management, Mrs. Boardley continues to expand Orbs Royal Treatment while mentoring aspiring event professionals. Mrs. Boardley leads a full life with her family and business. "Run your own race at your speed, and you will conquer." Mrs. Boardley is the author of "Moving at The Speed of Me" and Co-Author of several books.

To learn more, visit: https://www.orbsroyaltreatment.com

Email: info@orbsroyaltreatment.com

YOU ARE ENOUGH

It's All About Believing
By Audrey A. Boudreaux

"I would have lost heart, unless I had BELIEVED that
I would see the goodness of the Lord in the land of the
living..."
Psalm 27:13 (NKJ)

LIFE HAPPENS! Nobody stands at the altar of marriage planning a divorce, nor do parents expect to outlive their children. Nobody signs up to be abused, and nobody starts their dream job in hopes of being fired (unless they are an entrepreneur, lol). None of what happens in life is a surprise to God; it is only a surprise to us. When LIFE HAPPENS, and it will, please remember that delay is not denial, failure is not final, and you can begin again.

While I won't say that life has been easy, I will say I am thankful for my many experiences and lessons of survival. Walking through the pain, heartache, disappointment, and sometimes shame of life, I learned who I was and who I was not. My Faith muscles grew during my moments of doubts, insecurities, uncertainties, and fears.

I remember one particular season (yes, there have been several) that I wanted to run away from life. Yep, it's true. I wanted to run away, change my name, and start all over again. At some point, in the midst of it all, I began to encourage myself in the Word of God. I had to make up my mind to believe that I would not lose heart. I made the

[47]

decision and chose to believe that I could really live the life I prayed about. I then began to make it a daily practice of the following:

- I kept saying what I believed, not what I doubted.
- I kept the vision before me, repeating what I saw.
- I kept seeing myself as a finisher.
- I kept my eyes focused on the prize and not my past.
- I developed an arsenal of scriptures (words of faith and encouragement) and music that spoke to my heart. Words that reminded me that my life has purpose and that I am more than a conqueror.

I encourage you to create your own system or process now so that when you need it, and you will, it is there.

I want to remind you that you were created for such a time as this. That God has plans to prosper you and not to harm you. You were fearfully and wonderfully made. Do not, absolutely, do not throw away your confidence. All things, not some things, but all things will work together for your good. The Joy of the Lord is your Strength!! God hasn't given You a Spirit of Fear but of Love, Power, and a Sound Mind!! Rejoice! The Best Is Yet to Come! Keep Pressing, Keep Moving, Keep Getting Up, and Keep Showing Up!! Make up your mind that no matter what, you will not lose heart. After all, **IT'S ALL ABOUT BELIEVING…………YOU ARE ENOUGH!!**

BIO:

Audrey, an International Speaker and Coach, delivers life-changing messages that empower her audiences to do, to be, to grow and to believe more in their possibilities for winning in life.

Audrey is the Senior Pastor of New Hope Community Fellowship and is also the Founder and CEO of "BEYOND ALL BOUNDARIES INTERNATIONAL," a nonprofit organization that globally addresses the need for self-sufficiency.

Audrey and her husband Tony reside in Maryland. Audrey is working on her first book to be released in 2021.

IG@boudreauxaudrey FB: Audrey A. Boudreaux

YOU ARE ENOUGH

You Are Enough to… Leave Your Legacy!

By #BrandMaster, Martina Britt Yelverton

"...Then I hated all my labor in which I had toiled under the sun, because I must leave it to the man who will come after me."
Eccles 2:18
"...Fear God, and keep his commandments: for this is the whole duty of man."
Eccles 12

Have you ever thought about it this way?
If you don't do it, someone else with your similar journey won't; because you didn't?
Someone somewhere is waiting for YOU to show them they can!

Growing up as a chocolate girl amongst my grandmother's and mother's creamy caramel complexion cousins, I always felt my only related visual was my similarly melanated uncle. On my grandfather's and father's side of the family, I more easily related because we were all of similar complexions, except for the newest baby girl. Now, because I knew what it felt like to feel like an outsider, I loved on her feverishly, thinking I never wanted her to feel like I felt when I visited "the other side," as I called it.

YOU ARE ENOUGH

Now, while THIS may have NOTHING to do with why YOU are Enough to ...Leave Your Legacy, it speaks volumes to how YOU can change the trajectory of another's journey based on your perception of your own journey. I felt isolated, so I ensured that she never would. Not as long as she had me!

You have experienced something in this life that has left a scar, a mark, a forever brand on your memory that you need to revisit to begin your journey to Leaving a Legacy. Why? Because you and your story are ENOUGH to matter! AND that event, situation, tragic instance was meant to prosper you, not to impair you. Additionally, it wasn't meant JUST for you; it was meant for God to shine through you so others can know they can prosper through pain too.

A legacy is not just about money or possessions. Many of our Ancestors left untapped value for us to pick up and carry forward, distribute, elevate, and even recreate. That gentle spirit of a warm greeting when you first arrive, an embrace, a smile, a symbolic parting gift, or simply the aroma every time you visit - all are legacy elements you too can carry forward as your legacy. The value of something taught to you that you now teach to your children, nieces, nephews, cousins, or grandchildren is a legacy element they can then carry forward.

In Ecclesiastes, it repeatedly says, "in the end what you do on earth is meaningless, and that there is nothing new under the sun." Additionally, it says, "fear God and follow his commandment, that this is your duty." I say that the only way to ensure your legacy is carried forward is to follow your duty to love, love on others, and share YOU.

Know that you are valuable, your experiences have value, and that as parents, you are enough to leave your value as a legacy. I am deeply passionate about this because if we are to experience things and there is nothing new under the sun WHEN we get through an experience and learn from it, then and only then, Are We Enough to Leave Our Legacy of that experience! Do NOT underestimate YOU!

BIO:

My name is Martina Britt Yelverton, and I am a...

+ BrandMaster

+ CashflowQueen

+ Founder of the #1 Hire Your Kids Legal Tax Hack Movement

I help people who want help! If you need the help, I've been blessed to offer, follow me and select the bell for alerts when I go live on YouTube or Facebook!

FREE CONTENT is available at http://youtube.martinabrittyelverton.com.

If you've struggled as a #Parent, as an #Entrepreneur, as a #Brand or #HomeBasedBusiness owner, I can help you:

+ #GetYoASSetsInOrder

+ #GetBranded

+ #GetFound On Google

+ #GetPaid Daily

If you're serious, text "brandmaster" to 474747 TODAY!

YOU ARE ENOUGH

Paid & Free

By Latasha Brooks

*"The goal is to be PAID AND FREE, not BOOKED
AND BUSY."*
Latasha Brooks

As an entrepreneur, we have chosen to dedicate our time, energy, and resources into our own legacy instead of working for someone's else's. It is a difficult decision to make. The entrepreneur path comes with many challenges. It is a journey. One that is not a straight path. It has rough terrain, unpredictable curved roads, mountains, and hills. It is a difficult path to choose. Along the way, there are some excellent experiences, some bad and some ugly. I am an expert in business development, and I specialize in government contracts, motivational speaking, marketing and design, corporate training, and event planning. I am classified as a serial entrepreneur. How many of you are booked and busy? Do you know the definition of booked and busy? Booked and busy is when you have your calendar completely filled, and you are so fulfilled you don't have time for anything more. I recall in my early days on entrepreneurship, I saw a trend of booked and busy, and I wanted to be booked and busy as well.

I know many entrepreneurs that need to break the cycle of being booked and busy. But how? I will share with you how I did it. One day, I decided to write down the things that I value the most. I began to write down the conversation I was having with myself and put it on paper. So basically, I transferred my thoughts into visuals to create an understanding. I started to do just that. I wrote everything that came to me without giving it a second thought. This allowed me to convert what was going on in my mind to reality. I discovered I struggled with the internal conflict with being booked and busy. We must face the giant to defeat it. I could not miss this crucial step to transition from booked and busy to paid and free properly. My mind was made up, and there was no turning back. I wasn't going to spend another moment being booked and busy. Instead, I decided that paid and free was better suited for my lifestyle. It had fewer side effects and was tolerable.

My advice to anyone initiating a new journey, regardless of the path, just start. We often delay the start. You must take the first step, the next step, and just keep stepping in the direction of your goal to accomplish your dreams. Trust me, I know from experience. Don't delay. I took the first step to be paid and free by looking at my calendar and making a plan. Paid and Free is not easy. I am continually working very hard to maintain this status. Once my work is complete (I am Paid), then I am Free. Now it is time to ask yourself that tough question, do you want to be booked and busy or paid and free? You are Enough!! YOU deserve to be PAID AND FREE.

BIO:

Latasha Brooks is the author of Paid and Free Million Dollar Mission. Latasha is a serial entrepreneur and business coach with over ten years of experience helping other business owners. Latasha is the recipient of several awards, including the Iconic Woman Award in Virginia and the Outstanding Woman Award in Florida. A Florida native, she is a lover of crafting, traveling, and beaches. Coach Brooks lives in Virginia with her husband, two daughters, and two adorable guinea pigs. You can chat with Coach Brooks on Social Media at @moneybaggs623. You can visit her online at www.latashabrooks.com or www.paidandfree.com

YOU ARE ENOUGH

Dear "D.I.V.A" You Are Enough
By Serena Brothers-Mohamed

*"Likewise, teach the older women to be reverent in
the way they live, not to be slanderers or addicted to
much wine, but to teach what is good."*
Titus 2:3 (NIV)

The time is now because you are **Divinely Directed;** you have a
purpose.

Don't dim your light to let others shine because you want to be seen as
humble, not bold, bossy, or extra like you have been told probably
many times before. **D.I.V.A.,** you were created to shine bright. A star
can't dim its brightness to let the other star shine. The stars shine
bright amongst other stars as a constellation, so find your star crew.

You have talents, ideas, dreams, and visions that are just for you, that
would change the world and impact others. You were born with a
business, an invention, and a story to tell, so tap into your superpower.

Furthermore, you are an **Innovator.** The time is now for you to make
moves on your visions, dreams, and ideas. Don't let anyone talk you
out of it because it's your birthright. Furthermore, you hold your
legacy and inheritance in your womb and heart. The idea will allow
you to be a blessing to your family and a blessing to your others.

YOU ARE ENOUGH

You are **Victorious. D.I.V.A.,** your life lessons have placed you in a cocoon state. You took time to grow; now it's time to spread your wings and stand in your victory and be your authentic self.

You are a masterpiece. Adjust your crown queen **D.I.V.A.** Not one of your scars was in vain. It's your testimony. Your tears are just a sign you have lived and survived **Victoriously. D.I.V.A.,** Your time is now. It's no accident you are reading this because the stars in heaven have aligned for this very time. You are walking into your **Anointed and Appointed** season.

It's time to share what you learned in your cocoon stage as you were practicing the three p's Praying, Praising, and Planning even when life was not kind. You are now a master teacher of your story, so share it with the young **D.I.V.A.'s** watching you. It's time for a new thing, so spread your wings, my beautiful butterfly. **D.I.V.A.,** don't give all yourself away. Allow time for you to be poured into. Make time to practice the three r's Relax, Refresh and Release. Say this with me, "I'm **D**ivinely Directed, I'm an **I**nnovator, I'm **Vi**ctorious, I'm **A**nointed and Appointed, and I'm more than enough." So, the next time someone calls you extra or a diva, you should just smile because you know who You are. I am **D.I.V.A.** Phenomenally, that's me.

You are Divinely Directed

You are an Innovator

You are Victorious

BIO:

Serena Brothers-Mohamed is a dedicated educator and community leader. She encompasses empowerment through her accomplishments of becoming an author, wedding officiant, yoga and mindfulness instructor, Columbia Teachers College certified College and Career Advisor, and a transformative speaker. Of these accomplishments, one of her biggest is being the proud parent of Mark, Zaria, and Aaliyah and wife to her husband Mark of 25 years. Serena is the founder of Young, Talented & Gifted, a non-profit organization. Serena is also the co-founder of Staten Island S.T.R.O.N.G. HBCU College Tour and the recipient of the NYS Women of Distinction award.

YOU ARE ENOUGH

Overcoming the Storms
By Dr. Trina D. Brown

"Don't let unhealthy behavior hinder you from
walking into your PURPOSE."
Dr. Trina D. Brown

The most difficult thing is to believe in yourself when you come from a broken family. Once you understand you are not broken, it is easier for you not to look back at other people's mistakes. I had to learn how to forgive so I could believe. I've seen generational curses broken just by trusting what God said in Jeremiah 29:11: *"For I know the plans I have for you," declares the Lord, "plans to prosper you and not to harm you, plans to give you hope and a future."*(NIV) One of my favorite scriptures is III John 3:2: *"Beloved, I pray that in every way you may succeed and prosper and be in good health [physically], just as [I know] your soul prospers [spiritually]."*(AMP). I want you to believe in yourself; yes, I am talking to that child who never thought they could see themselves be happy, successful, and loving life without guilt. Even if life dealt you a bad hand, remember you can change the outcome by changing the way you see yourself. Do daily affirmations from this day forward, tell yourself I AM ENOUGH, I AM happy, I AM successful, I AM lovable, so you are open to receive all that you deserve.

"Sometimes, the hardest storms to get through are the
ones your soul needs most. Once the storm is over,
you will not remember how you made it through, how

*you managed to survive. But survive, you did. And one
thing is certain: When you come out of the storm, you
will not be the same person who walked in. That's
what the storm's all about."*
Dr. T. Brown

You can do all things through Christ, which strengthens you; If you
are going through a storm, speak to your storm right now, and hold on
to your faith. Matthew 17:20: *"Because you have so little faith. Truly I
tell you, if you have faith as small as a mustard seed, you can say to
this mountain, 'Move from here to there,' and will move. Nothing will
be impossible for you."* (NIV)

Make sure you walk into every day to make changes in the world we
live in so that you can be the change that you want to see. Live so that
your family can say you were a person that was DRIVEN BY
PURPOSE! Romans 12:2 *"Don't change yourselves to be like the
people of this world, but let God change you inside with a new way of
thinking. Then you will be able to understand and accept what God
wants for you. You will be able to know what is good and pleasing to
him and what is perfect."* (ERV)

I did not stop praying, no matter what I was going through, even when
I felt like giving up. No matter what you are facing right now,
remember prayer still WORKS (Winners, Overcomers, Rewarders,
Kingdom Success ~ **Dr. T. Brown**).

**Tell yourself YOU CAN! YOU WILL! I AM GOING TO MAKE
IT!**

BIO:

Author, Community Advocate for Healthcare & Humanity, International Speaker and Radio Host in over 180 countries, Mental Fitness Coach, Inventor, Evangelist/Prophetess, Founder/CEO Data Civility LLC and Neuro Pathic Trainers Foundation, Inc. division of Dr. Trina Brown & Associates. Dr. Brown has served on numerous committees and ministered with various organizations. Dr. Brown's mission is to educate and empower people about healthcare issues with dementia and its financial impact on families and communities. "Power and Greatness within the M.I.N.D." Mental Improvement Negates Deterioration. God-fearing woman who trusts the Lord.

(206)579-6308

tdbrown@neuropathictrainers.com

www.drtrinabrownspeaks.com

www.neuropathictrainers.com

Facebook: www.facebook.com/tdbrown7

Ingram: https://www.instagram.com/drtrinabrown

LinkedIn: https://www.linkedin.com/in/trina-brown-a0b9467

YOU ARE ENOUGH

Cultivate Your Greatness
By Linda Caldwell-Boykin

*"You were designed for accomplishment, engineered
for success, and endowed with seeds of greatness,"*
Zig Ziglar

Everyone who has obtained greatness didn't obtain it overnight. Subsequently, they started in seed form and cultivated that which was planted on the inside of them until that seed became a tree of greatness. You were created to have dominion, be fruitful and multiply in the earth. You have the potential for greatness down on the inside of you, and everything necessary to be productive and successful.

To manifest this greatness in our lives, many sacrifices must be made. You see, greatness never goes on sale. We must understand the cultivating process and what it means to extract from your passions and abilities during small beginnings. Seeds must be planted in soil, watered, and given sunshine for them to grow. Simultaneously, when the seed begins to grow, weeds will grow up with it. Weeds present the potential problem of choking the life out of the seed and stunting its growth. Therefore, pruning is inevitable so the weeds won't hinder the seed from sprouting into what it was intended to become. Many of us have not tilled the ground around the seeds God placed on the inside of us, allowing the greatness in us to lie dormant. When we understand the enemy of great is good, we will realize the importance of not settling for being average.

YOU ARE ENOUGH

Acknowledge and relinquish all enemies that constantly keep you living beneath your privileges, forfeiting your dreams and abandoning your goals. It's time for you to spread your wings and soar into who and what God intended. Having said that, let's get rid of procrastination, fear, doubt, laziness, and all negative self-talk that causes you to embrace mediocrity. These are enemies to your greatness. You must till the ground with hard work, preparation, commitment, dedication, and long hours of consistent and persistent efforts to cultivate your seeds of greatness. I can remember working the job that I literally hated going to every day. I always knew that there was something tugging on me to become an entrepreneur. After finding myself in total frustration, I decided to take a chance on myself and go after something greater. I had a passion for hairstyling; it was the one thing I could do for free on any given day and not feel slighted at all. I proceeded to take a leap of faith and go to cosmetology school. I vowed to myself once I was licensed, I would quit my job and become the entrepreneur God intended. Without fail, it happened; I was delivered from a paycheck to freely employ myself. Talk about being liberated! I'm now the proud owner of Salon Spirit, a safe haven where women relax, renew, and be restored. You owe it to yourself and those who are waiting on you to leap into your greatness. Your seeds of greatness are about to spring forth.

BIO:

Linda Caldwell-Boykin is an entrepreneur in Maryland. She is the proud owner of Salon Spirit, LLC, where she operates as the Senior Cosmetologist since 2010. She has accomplished great success in transforming lives with creative looks for over 20 years. Her profession has served as a catalyst for a greater purpose for those who have been broken and shattered by life's darkest moments. She is known for engaging conversations that inspire individuals to propel from the ashes and embrace their God-given greatness. Linda Caldwell-Boykin obtained a Bachelor's Degree in Ministry and is currently studying for her Master's Degree in Ministry at Virginia Bible College. She can be reached at Ambassador4ChristMinistryLCB@gmail.com

YOU ARE ENOUGH

Dating My Husband Again
By Leona Carter

*"Your awareness of the problem can't be bigger than
your actions to solve the problem."*
Leona Carter

I just finished having a huge argument with my husband. The reason we were arguing was not the reason we were arguing. I spent so much time trying to prove my point that I did not consider the person. I learned early in my marriage that building intimacy with my husband did not come naturally for me, really for two reasons. 1) I didn't know what building intimacy was, and 2) My body did not respond in a normal manner due to health issues. This caused a strain in our marriage and resulted in many nights of not having our needs met even after we made love.

My doctor confirmed, my lab test revealed I had Lupus and Rheumatoid Arthritis. I left the doctor's office with 13 new medications to start taking daily, including a shot in my stomach. The weight of that diagnosis felt like an elephant on my chest because it was hard to breathe.

After seven years of emotional and physical pain, the pain of staying the same was greater than the pain of change. I took steps to get my marriage back on track because it was spiraling fast and out of control.

YOU ARE ENOUGH

As a girl with a prayer and a plan, here are the steps I took, in this order, to turn my marriage around and learn how to build intimacy with my husband.

1. Pray and sincerely ask God to protect my heart while I fight for my marriage and teach me how to cover my husband in prayer while being covered. (This step alone took months before I could move to step 2)

2. Get honest about where I was because I can't fix what I don't face.

3. Release my husband from the expectations I had but never communicated.

4. Let go of majoring in the minors and trying to keep score.

5. Learn how to date my husband again.

6. Connect with my husband in the kitchen long before I connect in the bedroom.

7. Communicate my needs with curiosity, not accusatory.

Today, I am happy to share that we celebrated 25 years of marriage in September 2020. I love what our marriage looks like. We're literally living the marriage of our dreams. (Oh, by the way, I'm no longer on any medications.)

If my marriage can turn around, so can your marriage because You Are Enough, too!

You are enough to live a life with a marriage you love to go home to.

You are enough to be loved unconditionally.

You are enough to pursue your passion and have a great marriage.

You are enough to be held in the arms of the man who can't see himself without you.

You are enough for your husband to fall madly in love with you all over again.

You are enough to decide you are worth it.

The next time you pass a mirror, look at that beautiful woman looking back at you and tell her, You Are Enough.

BIO:

Leona empowers women to build intimacy with their husbands through the power of dating again. Leona is an International Empowerment Speaker, Best-selling Author, and Relationship and Intimacy Coach. Leona hosts Hey Coach Carter TV, where she talks with women who are building their business and their marriage. Married since 1995, Leona, and her high school sweetheart, Omarr, have six children and one grandson. Leona and her family moved from Seattle, Washington to Kalamazoo, Michigan for the tuition-based program called The Kalamazoo Promise, where her family was featured in the New York Times. Connect with Leona on social media at LeonaCarter.club.

YOU ARE ENOUGH

Ready or Not, Take your Shot
By Dr. Elizabeth A. Carter

"I am not throwin' away my shot."
Lin-Manuel Miranda

I stare at the application; the deadline is approaching. Every day like clockwork, the papers come out of the folder and are fanned across my desk like a new deck of cards. The requirements and instructions do not change, but my mind constantly does. With the initial excitement, confidence was whispering in one ear, "this would be a great opportunity," "would open doors to untapped territory," "this is your time.". But self-doubt was screaming in the other ear, "you are not ready," "you are not really qualified," "who are you to give advice that hasn't been tested by anyone but you?" Covering both ears, my response to myself was that this was the problem; you need experience to get opportunities, but need opportunities to get experience.

The daily ritual included adding a few sentences to my jumbled set of thoughts on my notepad, with the compilation ingeniously needing to describe an impressive solution. Would the selection committee consider my ideas interesting, innovative, or idiotic? Those reflections and incomplete answers ended each session.

Weeks go by; it is Sunday afternoon. The submission deadline is 11:59 pm that day. The folder is calling my name, and I decide defeatedly to wait until next year. If I don't submit, who knows? No one. If I do submit, who knows? No one. I made a note of interim projects I could do to feel more prepared next year, but who are we kidding? A box sits in my closet full of ideas and tasks I wanted to complete by some loose deadline that has long passed. I knew once I moved yet another aspiration from my 'to-do' folder to my 'maybe I'll remember what I said I was going to do to prepare' file cabinet, the thought, passion, and desire would be lost.

Even though no one else knows, I know.

It is 10:30 pm Sunday. A boost of rejuvenation overcomes me like a shock from a defibrillator. Can I get it done and submitted in 90 minutes? Pulling out the folder, arranging my thoughts, searching for the website link and contact names, I realize there are more questions I had not contemplated; will I finish this in time?

It is 11:30 pm. I must start transposing my answers to the application. Sweat on my forehead, fingers trembling trying not to make a mistake, tears in my eyes because I shouldn't have procrastinated and have now put all this pressure on myself….. I enter the recipient names and then press 'SEND.'

It was 11:59 pm Sunday when I pressed the button, but 12 am Monday was shown in my sent box. Was I late? Did I do all this work for nothing? I went to sleep with anxiety and accomplishment.

Late Monday morning, I received a response thanking me for my submission. It did not say I was late, and a boulder of relief was raised from my shoulders.

It does not matter if I get accepted or not, and I am overjoyed that I didn't throw away my shot.

BIO:

Dr. Elizabeth A. Carter is a finance leader, speaker, trainer, and author. With over 25 years working in Corporate settings, Dr. Carter's unique combination of financial acumen and knowledge empowerment has provided her the opportunity to lead, mentor and develop others.

Her company AAPPEAL, LLC, empowers women who feel unseen in the workplace to make their voice visible with tips, tools, and resources that illuminate their presence and increase the profits of their organization. Finding this passion provided her the platform to share her gift and continue her finance career.

Contact Dr. Carter

Website: https://www.eac-aappeal.com

Facebook, Twitter, Instagram – eacaappeal

YOU ARE ENOUGH

I am BRANDED BY GOD™ and So Are YOU!

By Kim Carter Evans

"Do not go where the path may lead, go instead where there is no path and leave a trail (of sparkle & glitter)."
Quote by Ralph Waldo Emerson (adapted by Kim Carter Evans)

The world, especially in the age of social media and virtual presence, will make you think you have to change, conform, and create a version of you that is unauthentic. The world will make you think you must follow the path and trends of everyone else. I also believed this. Even as I embarked on this journey, I thought to myself, "you don't have a brand; you don't even have social media handles or a website." "You have never even taken brand images other than the ones you use for your professional career." "you don't, you don't, you don't," I said to myself. I almost talked myself out of this opportunity to step into my calling, as so many of us do. Then God whispered in my ear, "my child, you DO have a brand. You are fearfully and wonderfully made. I have branded you. I only need you to walk in who I have created you to be."

Have you ever had that burning desire in your heart that just will not go away? This could be connected to your divine purpose and thus your God-given "brand."

YOU ARE ENOUGH

The brand that is authentically you is connected to God's divine purpose for your life. It is connected to your God-given talents. As you go about the journey of discovering your purpose in God, He will also reveal to you how He intends for you to use that purpose for a greater good, for His glory alone. It will not be for the glory of the "likes" you receive on social media. What makes you "you" is nothing physical; it is connected to your hopes, dreams, values, and morals. So many more of us are just drifting through life, attempting to be the carbon copy and second-rate version of either someone we know or someone we have seen on "the gram" rather than being the first-rate version of ourselves. Some even believe they do not have a divine purpose to live out on the Earth. No matter who you are, you were born with and for a divine purpose. The unique thing about the purpose that God has for us is it cannot be undone. Once God establishes His purpose for our lives, we cannot undo it no matter what we do.

> *"I know that you can do all things; no purpose of*
> *yours can be thwarted."*
> Job 42:2

As you step into your purpose, you will have to: Get comfortable with being uncomfortable. The day you become ok with not being "liked" is when "you" finally show up. You finally become authentically you. Know that you are enough to step into the starring role of your own movie and stop being an extra in someone else's. Choose to go where there is no path and leave a trail of sparkle and glitter. It is time for you to be who you were BRANDED BY GOD™ to be!"

BIO:

Kim Carter Evans ("the" KC Evans) excels in both her career as a corporate executive and an international speaker, author, and entrepreneur.

As a community advocate and leader, she dedicates her gifts and time to local non-profits and ministry. As a successful entrepreneur and brand manager serving high-profile clientele across the US, her clients have appeared in the NY Times, Black Enterprise, Washington Post, Ebony, and Essence. Clients have received national television media opportunities with BET/Centric, The Food Network, and all major news networks.

Ms. Evans holds a B.A. in Mass Communications/Public Relations and an M.B.A. in International Business Communication.

YOU ARE ENOUGH

Set Your Reminder. God Is Ready To Put You On-Demand!
By Avis Cherie'

"There is no power in testimoaning. The fire comes from the voice of your testimony."
Avis Cherie'

There is a Call-To-Action for Ground Breakers to accept and come out from under the veil of fear, hiding behind their stories and believe that You Are Enough!

Take a glance at everything around you, and where you envision your journey taking you. Allow yourself time to process and receive beyond what the eye can see, while keeping your feet planted in the fertile ground of your purpose. That is where God will fill your cup and give you the power to teach and lead others as they travail. Keep your thoughts focused on becoming the Servant Leader you never had because that is the lane where your path and steps have been ordered. Store up your strength so that when you are called to deliver, you will flow in your God-Given abilities.

Therefore, be intentional about where you decide to Break Ground and Plant your Visionary Seed. Pay attention to the details and sacrifice it will take to nurture, produce and birth what you have been laboring for all of this time. Your process requires patience and prayer because some things will require you to wait, while God prepares and develops you. During this time, you may feel stretched beyond your limits, uncertain of what is next, and even feel doubt creep in to deter you. In those moments, it is imperative to exhale toxicity, anxiety, and uncertainty, and inhale the power of the provisions created to help you navigate and continue to press full steam ahead. Be aware of what comes into your space to distract you and make you lose focus of your mission. Keen awareness will help you set attainable goals that will empower you, and keep your priorities in alignment with where you desire to be in life. Know the difference between things that nurture your vision and dreams and the things that rob you of your creativity. Never wait for someone to validate the cost and price you have paid to be Astonishingly Amazing despite the twists and turns in your journey. Your authentication comes from the Glory and Power of God's anointing on your life. Believe that who you are, and what you have been through sets you apart from everybody else. Never apologize for your unique gifts and skillsets because they embody everything you need, to SPEAK LIFE into someone's situation, be the voice for the voiceless, and empower people to believe in themselves.

Prayer, patience, and discernment keep you in a posture to receive powerful downloads of inspiration for self and others, and the stability to deliver. This will give you the freedom to fulfill your assignment and purpose in life, which will always solidify your seat at the table and enable you to make room to serve healthy portions to others. Lastly, never forfeit what God has placed in you and where God is taking you because your steps have been ordered and you have been preselected and are more than qualified for the job.

BIO:

Avis Cherie' is a Servant Leader and embraces her God-Given abilities to dissect the ails in one's life, uproot hope & transform lives. Her transparency about her own life and raw-edge makes her an ideal Accountability Coach, trustworthy and equipped to champion those ready to become Mentally Unstuck! Avis Cherie' has three Self-Published Books: "***The Price of Evolution Series (Paperback & Audio Book) and "Life After Covid-19: The Nasty Reminder, No Longer Business As Usual***", and her Inspirational Vlogs on YouTube. ***BACKGROUND:*** Avis Cherie' graduated Summa Cum Laude and holds a Master's Degree in Human Services and Mental Health Counseling.

www.avischerie.me

YOU ARE ENOUGH

It's Time To Walk In Your Gifts
By Kearn Crockett Cherry

"A man's gifts makes room for him and brings him before other great men."
Proverbs 18:16

Are you walking in the gifts that God has given you? If it is often said, when you do something that you enjoy doing for free, money will follow. Everyone has gifts and talents that are unique to them. No one can do something exactly the way another person would do it, especially when it is God-given gifts. Many of us take jobs or careers that do not allow our gifts and talents to shine. The majority spend years or a lifetime frustrated because we do not love what we do for a living. Over the years, our gifts become buried. Some gifts are never awakened.

Have you ever wondered why some people become rich at an early age? Many self-made millionaires and billionaires start operating in their gifts and God-given talents at an early age. Even when they are working in someone's company, they find jobs that allow their talents to shine. If they are not working a job that allows them to work in their calling, they typically will focus on it in their off-hours because this is when they are the happiest. Many individuals who are miserable or not making the income they desire are not focused on their gifts. They may desire other individual's talents, but they may spend years working a business that just doesn't truly satisfy their needs.

YOU ARE ENOUGH

You see, we are born with several gifts. Some individuals eventually tap into all of their gifts and talents. These individuals are operating at their highest capacity because they understand what they were called to do. They understand their gifting. They can collaborate with others who are also operating in their gifts. When this happens, amazing products, inventions, businesses, and relationships are born. As the scriptures say, you will be in the company of great men. When you learn to operate in your gifts, money will always follow.

It is your gifts that allow you to fulfill your vision. Our gifts are our supernatural abilities given to us by God. They allow us to serve and help others. These gifts will also allow us to achieve prosperity as well. Don't be like the servant in Matthew 25:14-30 who buried his talents (money) that his master gave him to make money and return it back to him plus interest. Your gifts are talents that are meant to be used. This is your time to walk in your gifts. Each year you should take time to write down your plans to operate in your gifts. If you are not sure what your gifts are, spend time in prayer or meditation and ask God to reveal them. I challenge YOU to step out in faith and walk in your gifts.

BIO:

Kearn Crockett Cherry is called the "Butts in the Seats Queen". She is a speaker, coach, entrepreneur, and #1 Bestselling author. She teaches on "Creating Your Own Profitable Event" especially virtual. She is the co-owner of PRN Home Care for over 24 years while in healthcare over 30 years. She is co-founder and director of Success Women's Conference with over 17,000 virtually. She is the founder of Power Up Summit and Level Up Virtual Summit. Mrs. Cherry is the visionary author for her book anthologies - "Make It Happen" and "Trailblazers Who Lead" I & II. She is co-author of "Women Inspiring Nations" Vol. 2. She has been featured twice in Essence Magazine as the "Comeback Queen". She often says, "When one door is close try the next one, if it's close go around to the back, if not Create Your OWN, but never give up."

YOU ARE ENOUGH

You Are Enough To Profit From Your Purple

By Joyce Chesley Hayward

In the movie "The Color Purple," we are reminded that you can't pass by a field of purple without noticing it. Purple is unique, special, royal, majestic. It stands out and causes us to stop and take notice.

It took a friend to point out that actually, I am 'purple.' As women, many of us are shades of "Purple," and our modesty and humility prevent us from recognizing it.

From my early days as a CPA in the U.S., and through helping small businesses as a bank loan officer, I saw the giftings in many business persons and how I could help them have profitable and thriving businesses.

So, I started my firm helping other businesses. My clients made more profits for their businesses, and I was able to take vacations, go for lunches and treat family and friends when I wanted. It was going great; life was good. I didn't realize I had a power (*or Purple*) in me. I just knew I had the propensity to help business owners understand what they were doing in relation to their finances, recognize their "purple," and profit from it.

And then, I met a wonderful man and fell in love – who lived in Bermuda. Well, off I went to start anew, at 40. After successfully working a '9 to 5' (really 9 to 9) for several years as the Accountant General of the Country and then in international business, I realized I was again being called to help entrepreneurs. So, I started my business again.

The more I help my clients, the more I see that it's not just the skill and expertise that I bring; it's also the unique way I bring it. It's all the shades of "purple" that I am called to be. It's the fusing of Joyce the CPA, the Reverend Doctor, the dancer, the wife, and mother, all rolled into one. It's the fusion of the business mind alongside the morals, ministerial ethics, creativity, God-Centered principles, and passion for God that makes me my brightest shade of "Purple." It's the ME that helps clients be all they can be and Profit from THEIR Purple! So, how fitting that my business came to be named Fusion4Business. I've come to understand why I was led to choose the colors orange and PURPLE for my business.

You may wonder if you can do it too; if you can leave a good job and step out on your own. You may be questioning if you can start over at whatever stage in life. I encourage you to KNOW you have "purple" in you. We are all made with a brilliance that will make others stop and pay attention. If you have an idea for a business, YOU CAN DO IT; pull out your "Purple" and let it shine.

Whoever you are, whatever you do, bring your purple to the table. That will help you be successful, and you too can Profit from your "Purple."

BIO:

Joyce is a Certified Public Accountant (CPA), a graduate of Georgetown University, and a member of Alpha Kappa Alpha Sorority, Inc. She is a speaker, coach, consultant, and trainer. After establishing a CPA firm in Maryland and holding senior positions in Bermuda, Joyce has launched Fusion4Business (F4B). Joyce is an ordained minister in the AME church with a Doctorate of Divinity, and she loves to dance for the Lord. She is also blessed to have two bonus sons. Check out F4B's programs at www.fusion4business.com, connect on LinkedIn https://www.linkedin.com/in/joyce-chesley-hayward-a7640a80/ or FB https://www.facebook.com/joyce.v.hayward to help you "Maximize Profitability for Your Small Business."

YOU ARE ENOUGH

Born To Shine!

By Judie Clark

*"Let your light so shine before men that they may see
your good works and glorify your Father in heaven,"*
Matthew 5:16

Did you know that you were born to shine? It is God's plan that you
shine so that others are encouraged to let their light shine. We all shine
in different ways. We shine when we show up for life with the zeal to
win, despite the odds. It takes courage to shine. There is a difference
between being modest and dimming our light so as not to intimidate
others. Marianne Williamson said, "You playing small doesn't serve
the world. There's nothing enlightening about shrinking so others
won't feel insecure around you. As you let your own light shine, you
give others permission to do the same."

Dr. Stacey A Maxwell said, "Do not allow others to diminish your
light due to their own fears…let your light shine so brightly, that you
illuminate a pathway for others to find their way out of the darkness!"

So let your light shine! During adversity, conflict, sickness,
depression, and discouragement, let your light shine! Be determined
that if you fall, you will rise again!

As you continue slaying giants and overcoming obstacles; stay
uplifted. Strive to maintain an optimistic perspective. How you
perceive situations plays a big part in how well you endure them.

YOU ARE ENOUGH

Although some will feel blinded by your light, refuse to dim your light!

Let us realize that as we continue to climb to greater success, everyone is not going to applaud us, as everybody cannot handle our success. Keep shining anyway!

Let us remember that there are blessings in our storms, and joy in our journeys. Let us feed our faith, so that our fears will starve to death. You have got what it takes for success. You've got the tenacity, perseverance, and the power to get back up when you fall.

Be encouraged that you are enough – you are complete; just as you are.

To maintain our shine, we must:

1. Be willing to let go of those who no longer add value to our lives. We must know and accept when their part in our story is over. Be encouraged that whatever leaves your life makes room for something better.

2. Be willing to nurture ourselves. Do the necessary self-care of rest, recreation, nurturing, etc. Continue to press past the pressure of staying the same. It takes courage and tenacity to change.

3. Develop wisdom that enhances your shine. **Proverbs 16:16 says:** "How much better is wisdom than gold, and understanding than silver?" Be willing to take instruction from those who are currently where you would like to be.

Unprecedented times calls for unprecedented faith. Accepting God's power **is the connector between fear and faith.** Tap into the seeds of power inside you, so when challenged, you will emerge strong. When you miss the mark, keep shining! Let your light shine so brightly that others will see the success that flows through your veins! This encourages them to seek higher levels of greatness!

Keep shining! Don't ever give up – no matter what!

BIO:

Judie Clark is an author, speaker, and poet. Her motto: "My former pain is going to bring gain to others!" She is also the Founder and CEO of Women Who Care Ministries. They provide domestic violence services and weekly meals to 7,000 low-income children. Memberships: Leadership Montgomery, Montgomery Village Rotary Club, Montgomery County Family Justice Center Foundation and Sisters4Sisters Network, Inc. She received an honorary degree from Montgomery College, MD, 2014. She also received the Sheroe Award in March, 2021. She studied Business Administration at Trenton State College, NJ. She is celebrated for her phenomenal comeback from hardships and philanthropic heart of service.

Email: sheinspires@yahoo.com

Linked in: https://www.linkedin.com/in/judith-clark-58070946/

Facebook: https://www.facebook.com/judith.clark.98

Instagram: @overflowqueen

Mobile: 301-651-1918

YOU ARE ENOUGH

Don't Shrink Back
By Tesha D. Colston

"The Rock cries out to us today, you may stand upon me, but do not hide your face."
Maya Angelou

I was standing in the pulpit alongside the other ministers. We were all worshiping when another minister whispered in my ear, "you were not meant to be in the front of the room; you were meant to be behind the scenes." I didn't think, at the time, that it would impact me as much as it did.

Have you ever had something hit you so deeply that it made you question who you were and what you carried? I have, and through that, I learned that when people speak out of their cup of jealousy and insensitivity, it can negatively affect you and cause you to hide if you are not careful.

No matter what "they" think or say, your value is not captured by anyone else's feelings about themselves or you. Their empty words mirror how they feel about themselves and not about you, and they are not important. What's important is what you think and what you say about yourself. Are you going to embrace what they think, or will you flip the script around, be bold, stand on the rock, and be your authentic self? I want to encourage you to "Stand tall, BUT do not be ashamed... Do not be ashamed of what you had to go through to get here!" – Apostle April Cofie

YOU ARE ENOUGH

Years later, a minister told me that God was saying, "You've become a "master at hiding" and it's time to stop hiding. There are women who are waiting for you to come out of hiding so that they can step into purpose." At that moment, I felt my whole spirit leap, and I suddenly had a desire to start doing and being and living in my purpose. In those few moments, God used one of his vessels to destroy the words of darkness against my life.

Sis, I want this for you. Jesus invites you to leave your hiding place and join him. "Your rock is Jesus, and He wants you to come to Him for whatever you need and be transparent with Him about your vulnerability." – Felicia Turner.

Sis, someone needs the authentic you and all that you carry. Someone is waiting for you not to be ashamed of what you had to go through to get to where you are RIGHT NOW! Someone is waiting for you to come out of hiding and call them into their authentic self; their purpose is calling you. Someone is waiting for you to be courageous and stand on the rock, unhindered and shameless.

Sis, in the name of Jesus, I break off of you any negativity that has caused you to go into hiding. I declare over you that you have been released, and those chains are broken. I declare that YOU have everything already in you to be the best version of yourself! There's no need to hide. The whole world is waiting, anticipating what you carry, and you are worthy of being seen! You are loved, you are complete, AND you deserve to have all that you desire. The Rock Cries Out to **YOU** Today, You May Stand Upon Me, But Do Not Hide Your Face!

BIO:

Tesha D. Colston is a Life and Financial Coach, Speaker, Christian Author, and Evangelist with over 15 years of experience in Christian ministry and 20 years of Corporate Training and Facilitation, Call Center Management, and Supervision Experience.

Tesha's passion is to teach women how to partner with God to create the life she loves to live. Her personal journey has given her unique messages full of compassion and simplicity, and she encourages women in a way that fosters growth.

She is the founder of Smart Money Sisters - teaching Christian women how to partner with God to master the money thing.

Website: www.TeshaDColston.com

www.SmartMoneySisters.com

Social Media: Facebook/Instagram/YouTube @TeshaDColston

YOU ARE ENOUGH

You Are Enough To Break The Cycle Of Generational Poverty!

By JJ Conway

"Life has no limitations, except the ones you make."
Les Brown

In 2009, I came home from a military trip to find my house sold, my stuff thrown out, and divorce papers to sign. That week I became a single military mom with over $845,000 of debt to my name, most of which was taken (and spent) by my ex-husband.

That year, I became a statistic I had worked so hard not to be; black single mom living on handouts and rearing a son without his father. Would my son become a statistic too? He was now the third generation afflicted by divorce and debt. Would my baby get sucked into the preschool-to-prison pipeline?

I wish I could tell you I had great faith, but it was shattered, and my prayers were the angry kind. I am so thankful the Lord covers our faults with grace. He led me to over a thousand scriptures that I call the "Biblical Blueprint for Building Wealth." He encouraged me that those scriptures wouldn't be there if His children were supposed to be poor.

I began to believe that God would get me out of this mess and showed my faith with works (James 2:20). I became the side-hustle queen, working multiple businesses in addition to my military job. I ran toward my creditors instead of hiding from them, assuring them I would pay in full one day, even if I could only pay one or two dollars at the moment. I scoured the library and the internet and learned how to make money work for me.

I broke the generational cycle of poverty, and so can you!

Whatever you are facing today, you can always improve and uplevel your life. It doesn't matter what your circumstances are right now. You can start the process of prosperity today simply by making a decision to live for YOUR future. Not the life your momma or your spouse want for you. Not doing what your job or your so-called friends guilt-trip you into doing. A future YOU create. When you decide to make this change, it won't take long to see results! You don't have to be unhealthy. You can break the generational curse of disease and build enough wealth to maintain your best health.

Anyone can break the cycle of generational poverty when they follow time-tested success strategies. These strategies are biblical principles, and I will give you the first one today:

Wallace Wattles taught that the hardest thing you'll ever do is stay focused on thinking about yourself as prosperous. This is the first step we must take to break the generational cycle of poverty and push back against a world that tells us we're worthless and will never be good enough. We must believe that we are worthy, constantly visualize ourselves as prosperous, and make a commitment to our future. When we do, everything changes! Doors begin to open, and opportunity finds you. This is how you begin to break the cycle of generational poverty.

I believe in you, and I believe in your dream!

BIO:

Janine "JJ" Conway was the first African American to serve as a physicist in the Air Force, retiring as a Lieutenant Colonel after 23 years. After returning from a military trip to discover her house sold, divorce papers, and over $845,000 debt to her name, she became a financial planner. JJ learned how to hustle and make money work for her quickly yet ethically. She now teaches others the same personal growth and financial management skills that allowed her to break the cycle of poverty and mirrors these principles when working with businesses to improve processes, people, and profit.

Instagram: http://instagram.com/JJKnowsTheWay

YOU ARE ENOUGH

You Are Enough for A Bomb Relationship

By Montrella S. Cowan, MSW, LICSW

"Love is, without question, life's greatest experience."
Napoleon Hill

In my work as a therapist, I too often come across black folks who have fallen captive to a false narrative of what it means to show and feel love. There are historical reasons for this, but we deserve so much more. I'm here to help you see the possibilities to be seen and loved the way you deserve to be.

Dating back to slavery, the Black Family has been through hell. Our families have been dismantled and disenfranchised. Our Black men have been castrated by society first and then by many women in their personal lives at home.

As for us, black women have long been viewed as one of only two binary objects: Either we're sex symbols, or we're "Strong Black Women."

Vulnerability be damned.

Why You Shouldn't Settle for "Struggle Love"

YOU ARE ENOUGH

Too many black women navigate their love lives as if their only choices are between being a "Ride or Die" or being eternally alone.

Somewhere along the way, we lost the willingness to be open and vocal about our desire for love. Privately, many of us are tired of being "Ms. Independent." We quietly long in isolation to be loved and feel safe letting our guard down.

While we've worked too hard to risk coming off as weak, we must find balance between strength and vulnerability if we're going to be happy and fulfilled in love.

You're already a successful career woman.

You're a great parent.

You're a valued friend and confidant.

If you're tired of doing *all things* alone, you can find and foster a loving and fulfilling relationship.

Using my Healthy Love Formula (L.U.V.) can help you get started building the muscle you'll need to move into the romantic relationship you deserve.

L is for **Letting Go**. This starts with past hurts and traumas that you have experienced. Why? Because these experiences have left us with negative perceptions of ourselves. Trauma truly will have us believe lies about who we are, such as *I am not worthy of love* or *I am not good enough.* Being a sexual assault survivor, I know that this is much easier said than done. Decide to release that victim identity and start living the real you TODAY.

You are loveable.

You are loving.

You are loved.

U is for **Unlock Your Heart**. Your key is forgiveness. Forgive yourself for any compromises that you have made of your own values, needs, and desires. Then, forgive others for your own benefit, not theirs.

V is for **Visualize**. Growth and change start with a mental picture and underlying belief before they're manifested in reality. Bob Proctor said, "If you can see it in your mind, you can hold it in your hand."

The struggle is real, but you don't need to struggle in love. It's time to break through that tough outer shell and learn to find comfort and confidence in your womanhood, vulnerability, and humanity. After all, you deserve a bomb relationship too.

BIO:

Crushing barriers to mental health and wellness through motivational speaking and therapy, Montrella Cowan is the founder of Affinity Health Affairs, a best-selling author and all-around survivor who inspires people to step into their greatness.

Hailing from Brooklyn, New York, Montrella was surrounded by a plethora of generational woes including, welfare dependency.

Raped at 14, giving birth at 15, and then losing that same daughter at 25 to Lupus has given Montrella an exceptional ear for listening, understanding, and working with clients.

If you're ready to smash the past and co-create your future, Montrella can show you how. Visit at Affinity411.com.

Trust God's Divine Timing
By Lisa J. Crawford

*"And let us not be weary in well doing for in due
season we will reap if we faint not."*
Galatians 6:9

In 2004, I was working as the concierge in a 4-diamond hotel. I loved my position because I was able to be of service to my clients. One day, my Director requested that I do some things for a sales manager coming in to assist. When I met her, I asked if she would be with us full-time. She explained that she was a part of the task force and traveled around the United States. If a hotel needed the skills she had, they would hire her, provide lodging, food, and pay her a contracted salary. I thought to myself, "Wow, I'm going to do that one day!"

As I continued to develop in the industry, I moved from concierge to catering assistant. I did both jobs for a while before being promoted to Executive Meeting Manager and, finally, Group Sales. During this time frame of twelve years, I experienced toxicity between my Director and me.

I experienced racism from clients who assumed I was white over the phone due to my speaking voice. When they came in for a tour, they would say things like, "Oh, I did not know you were Black." I had bouts of depression, sadness and I cried a lot within. The constant belittling of my abilities as a sales manager was more than I could stand emotionally, but I kept trying.

[111]

YOU ARE ENOUGH

It was not until I passed out for a second time that the Lord spoke to me and told me to fix the problem. I humbled myself and did just that. I acknowledged that I was not coachable because I allowed another person to make me feel like I was not good enough.

Together, my Director and I, through humbling on both sides: I became Sales Manager of the year. Five months later, I was let go because they were going in a new direction. During that time off, I wrote a book, lost my home and vehicle, and was homeless for thirty days. Things just looked terrible.

I kept my faith strong and met someone who told me about a job that wanted employees who used to work in the hospitality industry. I called and left a voicemail, and within a week, I was in training to become a leasing expert. I would be showing potential clients different apartment complexes to lease them.

I lived in five states in ten months. The following year, I became a Task Force Consultant. It took thirteen years of learning and developing to get to my heart's desire. God is faithful. He hears every single prayer that we have in our hearts. I did not quit! Do not faint while on the path of your dreams. You will win if you faint not!

BIO:

Lisa J. Crawford is the CEO of LJC Motivations, through which she has impacted souls around the world with her messages of hope, comfort, and inspiration. She holds over twenty years of experience in the Hospitality Industry. Ms. Crawford is a motivational speaker, self-love after trauma coach, and best-selling author. She holds a Business Degree in Organizational Management from Bethel University.

Her writings are aimed at encouraging women and freeing them of the silent screams they hold within. With firsthand experience of trauma emerging from abuse, Lisa wields her life story as a tool to strengthen the broken.

YOU ARE ENOUGH

Queen, Shine Bright Like a Diamond
By Min. Nakita Davis

"You are the light of the world. A city set on a hill cannot be hidden.[15] *Nor do people light a lamp and put it under a basket, but on a stand, and it gives light to all in the house.*[16] *In the same way, let your light shine before others, so that*[a] *they may see your good works and give glory to your Father who is in heaven."*
Matthew 5:14-16 (ESV)

When we were children, many of us loved to run, laugh, sing, dance, and play. We believed that we could do anything and be anything our young, innocent hearts desired.

We believed that we could fly.

Then one day, the world became not so innocent anymore.

Perhaps someone told us we could not *sing,* we could not *draw*, or we could not *dance*. Somewhere in the world, many of us began to believe the opinions and thoughts of others more than the spoken WORD of God over our lives.

YOU ARE ENOUGH

Instead of rising to the occasion and defeating the Goliath in our personal lives, many of us chose to shrink and sink into the background of mundane and common practice.

But Why?

Who said that we could not Shine Bright Like the Diamond God created us to be? Who said that we were to remain seen and not heard? Who said that our opinions, our thoughts, and gifts did not matter?

More importantly, when and why did we believe this?

Sister, my beautiful, fearfully and wonderfully made Queen, allow me to FREE you today in this very hour.

You Are A City Upon A Hill!

Sis, this is not up for debate.

You are Fearfully and Wonderfully Made.

You are the Head and Not the Tail.

Above and Not Beneath.

As a Believer in Christ, You ARE of a Royal Priesthood.

Royalty is in your DNA.

You are Blessed when you Come, and You are Blessed when you Go!

You are Blessed in the City and Blessed in the field.

You add sparkle, pizzazz, shine, and pop to every room you enter.

Your Value is more precious than Gold.

Your Voice ~ no matter how raspy, high pitched, or anything else in between, is melodic to the right listener.

You are the Key to breaking generational curses.

First in your family and then out into the world.

You are a Gift, a luminous light, and Hold the Power of Life and Death in your Tongue! You, my Queen, are a force to be reckoned with, and anyone who cannot get nor handle your *je ne sais quoi* (that's French Queen for *something- something*) they can just kiss…. Your lovely hands as you graciously pray for them.

"What did you think I was going to say?"

You see, Queen, you are priceless, gracious, forgiving, intelligent with an Amazing sense of humor to match.

You are Nobody's side piece or snack, Sis.

You are a whole meal with the soda on the side, and I AM Proud of You.

You have come so far from that little girl who may have been hurt, misused, and misunderstood along the way.

[117]

YOU ARE ENOUGH

Just like you may have lost yourself along the way...

You can, in this very moment, FIND YOURSELF along THIS WAY, Because You Are Enough!

Sometimes Sis, you just need another Queen who lost her way to help you find your way back to the hill.

You are a City Upon a Hill~ so Shine Bright Like a Diamond, and go be GREAT.

You are Worth it!

BIO:

Min. Nakita Davis is a 2x Presidential Volunteer Service Award Winner under Barack Obama's term, a 2019 AT&T Dream in Black Top 28 Future Maker, a 2020 Woman of Faith recipient, and awarded the 2021 Top 100 Successful Women in Business by the Global Trade Chamber. In addition, she is the Proud CEO & Founder of Jesus, Coffee, and Prayer Christian Publishing House LLC. The #1 Christian Publishing House in the Land, helping more than 110 Women Worldwide to become National/International Best-Selling Authors in

18 months. Her team helps Women of Faith to birth their Best-Selling books fast! Known as the Atlanta Book Hit-Maker, her firm helps women gain the visibility, authority, and credibility their speaker, author, girl boss business deserves by providing global virtual stages, marketing, media, and PR assistance. Recently added to her portfolio of Excellence: she adds The Women WIN NETWORK. Her network is 100% produced for Women by Women Who WIN on ROKU, Amazon Fire TV & more(100Million Reach). Min. Davis is married to her childhood sweetheart and lives with their 2 beautiful children in Atlanta, GA. Jesus is the Source of her Strength.

Stay Connected:

FB & IG @jesuscoffeeandprayer

Clubhouse @minnakitadavis

Website: www.jesuscoffeeandprayer.com

Let's Work Together~ email all inquiries or booking to:

info@jesuscoffeeandprayer.com

YOU ARE ENOUGH

Become Your Own Boss
By Monique Denton-Davis

"If you don't have peace, it isn't because someone took it from you; you gave it away. You cannot always control what happens to you, but you can control what happens in you."
John C. Maxwell

Becoming your own boss means that you are enough to stand in your truth. Be ok with who you are, overcome obstacles, fight adversities and live to tell about it. It means that you have filled your cup and now have enough to pour into others. Over the last three years, I have learned that I suffered from people-pleasing and "POF" Putting Others First. Those were things that I was doing because I just wanted them to be happy. It was a huge responsibility and a heavy load to carry. I knew it but wouldn't stop. Others knew it and encouraged me to stop, but I just could not bring myself to fully stop.

At that time, I felt that "no" was disrespectful. I felt that "no" would hurt others' feelings, and I felt that "no" would be selfish. I wanted to please them, even at the cost of hurting me. As a matter of fact, I did not realize how detrimental it was to me until I started changing my behavior, focusing on myself, and putting myself first. I stopped worrying about how others might feel. I stopped worrying about hurting others' feelings. You see, I found myself in a position where others had literally forced me out of their lives. Two people that I loved and still do. Two people that I was loyal to. Two people that I had sacrificed a whole lot of "me" to please a whole lot of "them" just to be left alone and tossed to the side when they had enough. Could you imagine?

The good news is...I was forced to BOSS Up. I was forced to focus on myself. I was forced to take control of my own life and put myself first. My serving them, no longer served them. So that chapter ended. My new chapter began.

Change and transformation can occur in one of two ways; either you're forced, or you do it on your own. I was forced, but the outcome still feels good!

You are enough; time to BOSS up.

Your storm will end. Your outcome will be great, and your future is bright. Have faith. Your faith is bigger than your current situation. Know that what God has in store for you is far greater than your current situation. Understand that the prize is in the process. The process is to prepare you for new beginnings, new chapters, new revelations, new blessings, and a new season.

Take control of your life now. There is no hero coming to save the day. Become your own hero, become your own BOSS. BOSS up and save yourself. My BOSS journey is full of laughs, heartbreak, lessons, and progression. Becoming my own BOSS was a journey to self-awareness, self-discovery, and self-love. My BOSS allowed me to lead and share with others so they can find their BOSS before being forced.

BIO:

Monique Denton-Davis is a sought-after motivational/TedX speaker, certified life transformation coach, and author of several best-seller books. Monique is the Founder & CEO of Embrace Your CAKE, LLC, Life Coaching. Focusing on Confidence, Attitude, Kindness, and Excellence.

For over 20 years, Monique has held numerous leadership positions in the human resources field, including human resources director, training and recruitment director, executive-level recruiter, and corporate trainer. Utilizing all of her experiences when working with clients, she strategizes their personal lives and careers. She believes that self-awareness and empowerment allow women to uncover their true potential.

YOU ARE ENOUGH

You Are Enough - To Overcome Adversity

By Dr. Toscha L. Dickerson

*"Enter through the narrow gate. For wide is the gate
and broad is the road that leads to destruction, and
many enter through it."*
Matthew 7:13

How do you find your way when faced with adversity? How do you overcome some of the lowest moments in life? You find your way by making a conscious decision to move past your hurt and pain. You decide to change your current situation by recognizing you may need help. It takes a strong person to ask for support during their most difficult times. Finding your way is a process that is not easily navigated overnight. It will take time to get acclimated to a new way of thinking and living.

The first step in the process of finding your way through adversity is changing your mindset and accepting what God has allowed. In most difficult situations, we tend to ask God the question, "Why Me"? When we ask that question, it sends the message that you are more focused on your circumstances than God Himself.

A more appropriate question to ask is, "God, what do you want me to learn from this situation?" Maybe God wants you to trust Him more. Maybe He wants you to focus your attention on something other than what you have been doing. Either way, each difficult situation has a lesson that you can learn something from. It is your responsibility to determine what it is that God wants from you.

Focusing on the positive things in your life and showing gratitude is another step towards overcoming adversity. Although difficult moments can seem as if life is too hard to bear, there are many things to be thankful and appreciative of having in your life. Just knowing that God did not bring you this far to leave you is enough for you to keep fighting and not to give up. Sometimes all you need to do is to show up consistently every day.

Unexpected events will happen in life, and there is no way around them. The way you handle and respond to difficult situations is very important. The decisions you make can determine the trajectory of your life. Ensure you are taking the time to examine the entire situation. If the situation is an uncontrollable one, such as death, illness, or job loss, God is still in control and is aware of it all. Pray and ask for strength during this time. However, if this is a situation that you have the power to change, then make every effort to do so.

Approaching adversity is like looking at a glass half empty or half full. The hardship is still there, but the way you perceive the problem will make a difference in your life. You have the choice to view the problem as an obstacle or as an opportunity. When you choose to view it as an obstacle, you find yourself placing limits and restrictions on what can and cannot be resolved. However, when you choose to view the problem as an opportunity, you begin to see the possibilities and develop solutions to overcome that situation.

BIO:

Dr. Toscha L. Dickerson is a Strategy Coach, Best Selling Author, and Professor. She is an expert panelist for Houston Business Journal Leadership Trust.

She received her Doctorate in Business Administration with a specialization in Global Operations and Supply Chain Management at Capella University.

With numerous honors and certifications, Dr. Dickerson has committed 20 years to assisting others in their personal and professional development. She helps women reduce stress, explore self-discovery, and gain clarity in goal setting to live an empowered life.

She inspires and empowers women to move past their fears and live a self-sufficient life.

YOU ARE ENOUGH

Believe It and You Can Achieve It!
By Patrina Dixon

"And All things, whatsoever ye shall ask in prayer,
believing, ye shall receive."
Matthew 21:22 KJV

The time is now! Believe, and you shall receive. For someone to believe in you and your vision, you have to first believe in yourself. I am learning more and more that "I Am Enough." Depending on which room I was in, I didn't always feel like I was enough. I was either the only black person or only minority person and felt the need to "prove" I belong in the room instead of just being the queen that I am. I have a new sense of walking proudly in my zone of genius. Now that I own my own business and can decide which rooms I am in, I always feel like I am enough.

Being the CEO of my business has given me freedom in so many ways. You can be whatever you want to be; the key is starting. Don't wait until things are perfect. Perfection and evolution will happen in time. The reason I like the scripture Matthew 21:22 is that it reminds me, as a believer, all things are possible. I remember being ashamed to tell my story but then later realized that my story contributes to why I'm doing exactly what I am doing. Now I take pride in telling my story as people resonate with it, so as Dr. Cheryl Wood says, "Your story is not for you, it is for someone else," so now my tests are a part of my testimony. I have begun sharing my story more and more to help others. Once I recovered from being a spendaholic with jacked-up credit and no money saved to overcoming through transformational experiences, coupled with financial certifications, now my money story fuels me as a finance coach. I am here to tell you, YOU ARE ENOUGH, and once you believe, you will achieve.

BIO:

Patrina Dixon is a Personal Finance Expert, Certified Financial Education Instructor, Award-Winning Author, International Speaker, Executive Producer, and Podcast Host. I am also a wife, mom, and child of God. My team and I have facilitated financial workshops for individuals of all ages across the world, from CT to GA to TX to Trinidad and Tobago. Our financial workshops have helped transform lives by helping our clients begin or increase their savings accounts, increase their credit scores, and earn extra money with side hustles. I have been featured on FOX61, Black Enterprise, Experian, Yahoo Finance, and Real Simple.

You are Enough for Making Self-Care Essential

By Jacqueline R. Duncan

"Self-care is never a selfish act—it is essential and is simply good stewardship of the only gift I have, the gift I was put on earth to offer to others and that gift is--- myself"
Jacqueline Duncan

A blossoming flower emerges from the ground, moving towards the light of the sun's rays. It opens gently yet confidently, aware of its innate beauty and strength. As it emerges, the surrounding environment shifts at the impact being made, all because a blossoming flower is blooming. We, too, have been created to shift and alter our environment as we navigate successfully through the challenges, trials, and tribulations we face, resolutely to impact the world around us.

A key to giving your best self daily is regularly practicing self-care, taking care of yourself to be healthy and well in your spirit, mind, and body to care for others and do all the things you desire to do daily. Self-care is that safety tip they give when you travel by plane, "put your mask on first...". Self-care is not selfish, but it is essential! You must show up for yourself first to show up at full strength for others.

Self-care is all about you. You are in control, and you get to decide what self-care is for you. Is it going to the spa, watching movies, reading, writing, coloring, working with your hands, biking, hiking… there are no limits. The objective is that you feel cared for, refreshed, renewed, energized, and ready, spirit, mind, and body to give your best.

Let me encourage you that even when time or location may not be optimal for full-on self-care, a simple breathing exercise can relax and refresh you. Try it. Take a moment to relax, close your eyes, and take a few slow, controlled breaths. Breathe in through your nose, and exhale out through your mouth. Repeat a couple of times, and on the final time, end with a happy thought and a smile, or tell yourself a joke and then laugh out loud. I hope you feel a little lighter.

Meditation, journaling, "I Am" affirmations, and prayer are also great sources of self-care revitalization to bring you peace, joy, and a sound mind.

Do what you enjoy doing. Be inspired to make self-care a part of your daily, weekly, or monthly routine so that you can enjoy the many wonderful benefits that it brings from positive thinking, a healthier lifestyle, a victorious perspective, a focused mindset, and the energy to do whatever you need or desire to do.

Remember, self-care is essential for your overall well-being. We all face challenges in life, but we can control how we respond. Making self-care a way of life is a priority, not a luxury. Setting your mind on caring for yourself will change the trajectory of your life, revealing the authentic you and that who you are is good enough. Self-care is essential!

BIO:

Jacqueline Duncan is a renowned inspirational speaker, pastor, author, and entrepreneur. She is passionate about encouraging women to discover their purpose and is committed to providing them with the tools of information, education, and inspiration. Jacqueline is the owner of Leading Ladies of Integrity Inc., a Pastors' Wives Organization and Purpose Pusher Inspire Coaching LLC. She is the host of The Jacqueline Renee Show, and along with her husband Apostle Phillip Duncan, she pastors In His Presence Praise and Worship Temple in Maryland. A Clarksville, Tennessee native, Jacqueline is the proud mother of one adult daughter.

YOU ARE ENOUGH

You Are Enough To Overcome The Unknown Zone!

By Dr. Monique Flemings

"Sometimes you find yourself in the middle of nowhere, and sometimes in the middle of nowhere you find yourself."
Anonymous

"Spotty development. His development is spotty. There are some areas where his development is on track, and then there are some areas of development exhibited that are well over his chronological age. We call this spotty development. There are many reasons why we see this in children."

I could hear those words ringing in my head over and over as I drove some 50 miles from the city back to our home. That conversation left me numb. I completely understood the terminology and the neurodevelopmental information that was shared. As an educator in pediatric developmental stages, I was aware of the theory and stages of neurological development. I was about to understand this journey from a completely different perspective.

That ride home was the absolute longest ride of my life. With all my fears rushing to my face in the form of tears, my head pounding, my heart broken, my voice silenced, all in one moment, my entrance into

[135]

the unknown zone was granted, and I was not excited about the invitation. I was being thrust into the unknown zone.

There were so many emotions that swept over me. The unknown zone is full of mixed emotions, and I felt like the very foundation of my life was ripped from underneath my feet. I felt this place of uncertainty was unfair and unnecessary. I was feeling every bit of Abraham's wife Sarah from the Bible on this unknown, unwelcomed, uncertain place called transition. No, ma'am, I did not sign up for this at all.

Have you ever found yourself in the unknown zone? Have you thought to yourself, "How will I get through this life-altering experience?" Can I remind you that you are enough to get through this unknown zone and win! As much as it feels like you will be buried alive, allow me to encourage you with what I learned in the unknown zone.

1. The unknown zone showed me that at my core, I was a warrior and stronger than I could have ever imagined. My life had prepared me for this unknown zone, but I was unaware of the life lessons of preparation.

2. The creative genius within me was awakened. Unwelcomed realities birthed miracles of creativity that would have gone unnoticed if not for the unknown zone.

3. Having a tribe of faith-filled friends is crucial. When you cannot speak words of faith, your tribe becomes your CPR-your cardiopulmonary resuscitators. They speak life over you.

4. God is the God of the unknown zone. There is absolutely nothing that takes Him by surprise. He is with me and will never leave me. The ride may be very bumpy and tumultuous, yet the God who loves me unconditionally has not left the ship. I may not see Him, but He is there and still in control.

The unknown zone became my greatest teacher. Be encouraged, beloved. The unknown zone is necessary for your development, and you will arise from this stronger than ever!

BIO:

Dr. Monique, the Transitions Dr., has a diverse background as a physical therapist, minister of the gospel, and educator, which allows her to serve people with a unique perspective. An international speaker, coach, and author, her practical yet thought-provoking approach to solutions push transformation through understanding transitions.

She has served as the Director of Clinical Education and Adjunct Professor within her profession of Physical Therapy. Dr. Flemings' most recent book, *Mastering Transitions,* is a powerful tool providing language for navigating through seasons of transitions. Dr. Flemings serves as the Director of Affiliate Churches for the All Nations Collective.

YOU ARE ENOUGH

When Your Value Is Clear, Your Decision Is Easy!

By Dr. Jonas Gadson, DTM

"Beloved, I wish above all things that you may prosper and be in health, even as your soul also prospers!"
III John 1:2

There are three kinds of people…Those who make things happen, those who watch things happen, and those who wonder, "What happened?" I am a person who makes positive things happen, and I believe that you are too!

BONUS FROM JONAS

"You are a manuscript that has not yet been published. You are a poem that has not yet been composed. You are a song that has not yet been sung. You are a dream that has not yet been fulfilled. You are a vision that has not yet happened. Your future has not yet come to pass. You are a miracle waiting to explode!"

"God made you an original! Don't you dare die a cheap copy!"

"You Are Next In Line For A Blessing! Don't Get Out of Line, Don't Detour, and Don't Let Anyone Cut In Front of You! It's Full Steam Ahead! Whatever you focus on the longest will become the strongest!"

YOU ARE ENOUGH

Mr. Warren Buffet, a billionaire, was asked, "What is the greatest investment for the 21st Century and beyond?" They expected him to recommend stocks and bonds, but he said that the greatest investment is personal development and public speaking.

When I started working at Eastman Kodak Company, I would go to the learning center two hours before work to improve my skills. I looked through the book titles on the shelf…President, Manager, Supervisor until I got to employee. "This book is for me!" I had been taught to be a good employee; to get a good education, get a good job and work for one company for life! I discovered that there was no job security, but there is skill security! The more skilled you are, the more secure you are!

I have invested over $100,000 in my personal and professional development. Recently, someone asked me, "Dr. Jonas, Are you working hard on yourself to get somebody?" I said, "No, I am working hard on myself to be somebody!"

My Four-Step Personal Development Process helped me, and I believe that it will help you, too!

1. Education: Educate comes from the Latin word meaning; To lead and draw out the gift in you! Bonus From Jonas: "If you cheat yourself in your preparation, it will show up in your presentation!"

2. Inspiration: Now is the time that people need inspiration and a message of HOPE: Having Only Positive Expectations for You! "You can't do what I can do, and I can't do what you can do, but together we can do great things!" Mother Teresa.

3. Transformation: Move away from change to transformation! Change is temporary, but transformation is permanent. It doesn't matter how many legs a caterpillar has or how fast it can run. It will never fly until it is transformed into a butterfly!

4. Motivation: Now is your time to get up and get going! To live your dreams, your goals, and your aspirations, "Dare To Dream And Then Do It!" Congratulations on investing in the most important person on the planet YOU!

BIO:

Dr. Jonas Gadson, DTM, known as "Mr. Enthusiastic!" is an International Motivational Speaker, Corporate Trainer, Radio Personality, Author, and Expert Communication Coach. He worked for two Fortune 500 companies, Xerox Corporation and Eastman Kodak Company. At Eastman Kodak, he trained over 8,000 employees from 69 countries and earned the Trainer of the Year Award! He spoke at the Wonder Women Tech Virtual Summit in London, England, and has a Doctorate Degree in Theology. He was inducted into the Beaufort High School Alumni Hall of Fame for distinguishing himself in profession, leadership, and service. He has a chapter in two books, "Make It Matter!" and "I Am A Victor!"

To get your FREE gift, Go to http://www.jonasbonus.com(585) 703-9547. jg@jonasbonus.com.

   @jonasbonus2021

YOU ARE ENOUGH

You <u>Really</u> Are Enough!
By T. Renee Garner

"What you seek is seeking you."
Mawlana -al-Din Rum

You have the guts to take a peek at your dreams and go for IT! You must trust you are ENOUGH. When life just treats you wrong and yes, life was designed to test you. You must remember, You are Enough! Don't let anyone take "you are enough" away from you.

The emotional rejection, the feeling of being alone and the realization of abandonment are real heavy burdens of emotions that were designed with the intent to weigh you down. These are the mental emotions that affect your heart and what flows out of your heart are real emotions that affect your entire life. Believe in You and that You <u>really</u> are enough!

With all of you might to become aware and understand the reason why you felt reaching your dream became hard and cruel. Let me help you; you must hold tight because that feeling you felt was a trick robbing your right to believe that you are enough. As if something was trying to hide "You Are Enough" from your very own sight. Do You <u>really</u> have faith? Yes, of course, you do! Look in the mirror at the reflection of beauty and intelligence inside you. It is your right and by your faith that you see that You are on Fire.

YOU ARE ENOUGH

Let's go Higher! So, what is next? You are qualified and now justified to experience the kingdom of El Shaddai, the Almighty God.

Wait! Who is this Almighty El Shaddai? He is the God who is **more** than enough.

Yes, El Shaddai, the God with more ideas, abundance, more love, money, more of everything needed to succeed in life. Chile, recognize you have always been enough! and now the God of **"More"** is knocking at your front door!

Allow me please to introduce you right now to the God who is **More** than Enough. You meet God Almighty, El Shaddai, through a person by the name of <u>Jesus Christ</u>. So that you will know you <u>really</u> are with the God who has all sufficient tools and *is more than just a friend.* Would you join me in a quick prayer as the journey begins? According to Romans 10:9-10, the faith prayer of salvation, it is not tough to introduce you to the God who is More than Enough. Simply say,

"Jesus is LORD," and I believe in my heart that God raised Jesus from the dead, and <u>I am saved</u>. [10]For it is with my heart that I believe and are justified, and it is with my mouth that I profess my faith and are <u>saved</u>.

You must trust always in yourself. Being strong in your knowing that you are saved and truly filled with honest integrity because you are confident and You are More Than Enough!

BIO:

T. Renee Garner

Inspirational Speaker of Salvation

Contact and Request Press Release Kit

TreneeInspires@gmail.com

www.treneeinspires.com

"No eye has seen, no ear has heard, and no mind has imagined what God has prepared for those who love Him" – 1st Corinthians 2:9 (NLT)

<u>YOU ARE ENOUGH!</u>

To create and dominate.

God who purposely placed you to live on earth has given you the ability to Dream Big!

God's great work on the inside of you.
You are the apple of God's eyes and the absolute heartbeat of God.
Every time God sees you,
God is satisfied because you were born with all of His tools and Love,

YOU ARE <u>*MORE*</u> THAN ENOUGH!

Book T. Renee Garner: treneeinspires@gmail.com

YOU ARE ENOUGH

Pain to Purpose
By Dr. Chere M. Goode

"For nothing will be impossible with God."
Luke 1:37

"Keep your faith. Trust in the strength of God. Keep rising and give yourself permission to feel and heal. Be kind to yourself and perform daily self-care."

I know all too well feeling like I was not enough to make it through disappointments and tragedies in my life. I can recall times of wanting to quit and give up on everything when life hit me so hard that I could barely breathe. Aug. 22, 2020, and Feb 17, 2021, struck my life with the indescribable major losses of my youngest son Jordan Alexander Cofield at the age of 20, followed by the death of his father and my ex-husband Jeffrey Cofield at the age of 52, not even six months apart. The sting of grief will stop you cold in your tracks, put a heavy burden on your heart and spirit, leaving you feeling defeated. However, by keeping your faith and staying in prayer, God can and will help you through the worst times of your life and remind you that you are enough and will never give you more than you can bear. Being enough does not mean you have to be perfect. You can be perfectly flawed, broken, hurt, and still be enough. You can have waves of emotions that fluctuate day to day. The important thing to remember is that each day you rise is a blessing because it is another opportunity to feel, heal, learn more about yourself, and rewrite the narrative of your life. Each new day is a do-over to fix what you did not like about the day before.

[147]

YOU ARE ENOUGH

Just keep rising. Do whatever it takes to feel good, whether it be putting on a nice outfit with nowhere to go, doing a selfie shoot to feel good about yourself, or putting on upbeat music and dancing around by yourself.

Serving others is also a good way to shift your focus from your care and worries to focus on others' needs. Reach out to your support systems and if you do not have one, reach out to a professional therapist. A professional therapist can help you work through your feelings, aid you in healing, and provide the support you need. There is no shame in getting the help you need to be whole and well mentally, physically, emotionally, and spiritually. Be more determined to win than allow life occurrences to deter you from your purpose. Be brave and boldly continue in your life journey. Take one day at a time and move step by step. Just keep moving forward. Troubles only last a while, and even the pain you may experience from time to time will become more bearable as time passes. Create and recite a daily mantra to repeat to yourself to remind you why you should keep pushing to propel you forward with your daily activities and goals. Remember You Are Enough!

BIO:

Dr. Chere M. Goode is the Founder/CEO of Total Harmony Enterprises and Make Me Over Wellness. Goode is a mother, caregiver, and the Creator of the Annual RECHARGE Health, Wellness, and Fitness Expo. Goode has been a Licensed Practical Nurse for over 30 years and is Nationally Certified in Hospice and Palliative Care, an area she currently specializes in. Goode is a 5-time #1 Best Selling International Author, Speaker, and Wellness Coach and an American Heart & Stroke Association Ambassador/Spokesperson. Known as the RECHARGE Strategist, Goode teaches professional women strategies for self-care to recharge their Mental, Physical, and Emotional batteries for success in life and business through her 8 Recharge Pillars of Self Care.

YOU ARE ENOUGH

Your Vision is Your Victory
By Mijiza A. Green

"Then the Lord answered me and said: 'Write the vision and make it plain on tablets, That he may run who reads it. For the vision is yet for an appointed time; But at the end it will speak, and it will not lie. Though it tarries, wait for it; Because it will surely come, It will not tarry'."
Habakkuk 2:2-3

God had given you a vision of your future in plain sight, during a daydream, while you are sleeping, or perhaps even in mid-thought. This image has popped in your head, but you have ignored it. You have ignored it because it seems like it's too big, too far to reach; you might even believe you are not qualified for this vision to be manifested. Today I say to you, YOU are enough, right where you are. All that you have been through or might even be going through, YOU are enough. You are still loved; you are still worthy, and you are more than qualified. Through the storm, God gave you a vision as a reminder of where He wants to take you, but He is waiting for you to surrender, waiting for you to say YES. Saying YES requires a few things of you. First, you must take an inventory of what and who you are connected to. Do you understand you can be blocking your blessing because of your connections? God says release it, but you choose to stay connected like Wi-Fi. Stay connected to people and things that add to your value, lift you up, and that you can learn from.

[151]

YOU ARE ENOUGH

Second, devote your time, attention to things that build you up, not tear you down. Social Media is the Billion-dollar distraction to your vision. Do not place your value or validation on how many likes you get; use it as a platform to share your story or send words of encouragement. Use it to IMPACT, INSPIRE and EDUCATE all who see it. And lastly, write the vision down, so you do not forget it to reflect on it later. But writing it down signifies importance; if God gave it to you, it is worth writing it down because the vision is for the future. This future is not just yours; it's for the future of your children, grandchildren, and the next generation.

Make it so that someone else may follow in your steps, may use it to empower others. This vision God has given you is the victory that is already won. You now have to believe that whatever you have been through or still going through is only to make you stronger and wiser. The arrows of sickness, death, depression, troubles, trauma, and destruction that are fired at you are not there to destroy you; they are there for you to grab hold and fire back. Allow each one to be a lesson and motivation to be prepped and pushed into your Purpose. God has a plan and always had a plan for your life, no matter what you have been through. So, my friend, write it down, make it plain, so that the next generation will be able to run and spread the Good news because you said YES to your vision to your victory. You are enough, you have been enough and will always be ENOUGH! Trust HIM!

BIO:

Mijiza A. Green, Founder, and CEO of Planting Seeds Community Outreach and The Wellness Purse. Both created to Impact, Inspire, and Educate teen Girls and Adults through mental health and wellness coaching. Mijiza is a Bestselling Author, Inspirational Speaker, Mentor, Coach, and Consultant. Her Life's purpose is to share her story to empowering the next generation of leaders. Mijiza is the mother of three boys, stepmom to one daughter, and NaNa to two grandchildren, all while pursuing a second degree in Psychology at Morgan State University. Meet her at http://www.thewellnesspurse.com for more information or testimonials.

YOU ARE ENOUGH

You Are Enough To DOMINATE Your Emotional Currency!
By Brittany Greene

"But he said to me, "My grace is sufficient for you,
for my power is made perfect in weakness." Therefore
I will boast all the more gladly about my weaknesses,
so that Christ's power may rest on me. That is why,
for Christ's sake, I delight in weaknesses, in insults, in
hardships, in persecutions, in difficulties. For when I
am weak, then I am strong."
2 Corinthians 12:9-10

The goal is to break generational curses......To teach the next set of leaders and gurus the things we didn't know growing up and keep up with the changes going on in society. The goal is to set the people we love up for success. However, it starts with the mind! For ages, we have been torn down, forced into silence, deterred, or kept in certain boxes so that we would not explore and enhance that wonderful brain that God has given us.

But I ask you now...How can you pour into others or walk in your purpose from an empty cup? I know first hand! After being fired, losing everything, being homeless, and giving more to everyone else than I did myself, I felt depleted and defeated. I knew there was more to me than struggling to survive, but I didn't quite know how to unlock it. That's when I discovered my emotional currency, and I want to help you discover yours.

[155]

YOU ARE ENOUGH

Our mind either allows us to attract more abundance to us or repel the very thing we want….away from us. How do we become magnets to what we desire and receive the abundance that is our BIRTHRIGHT? It starts with these three things!

1. **Be definite in what you want:** Think about what you want and WHY! The most important part is your why because that's what will keep you going when life throws its blows. Ask yourself: What is most important to me? Why am I striving for freedom?

2. **Get in your head before anyone else does**: When I wake up in the morning, the first thing I do is feed and pour into myself to get ready for all the day has for me. Here are some resources that have helped me over the years [I hope this helps you as well]. Also, give yourself time to find your own groove for what works for you but explore!

   a. Morning walk: Nature is good for the soul

   b. Read self-development books: Master your emotions [Thibaut Meurisse], Think & Grow Rich, The Four Agreements, the Secret [Movie on Netflix as well]

   c. YouTube channels: Abraham Hicks [Law of attraction || pick me ups], Les Brown [inspiration], & Lisa Nichols.

3. **Don't QUIT!:** emotions range from day to day. Life will happen, and intrusive thoughts will come, but you have to make a conscious decision to be bigger than anything sent to destroy you. Remember, things are working for you rather than to you!

Lastly, be patient as your growth is NOT an overnight process!

BIO:

Brittany Greene is the founder and CEO of Crowned Financials. After losing everything and having to rebuild her credit three times, she made it her mission to close the gap and provide the financial literacy and credit education missing from the home and school system! Today Brittany has been seen on Yahoo Finance, Yahoo News, NBC, FOX, and Buzzfeed. She reaches the community through books, courses, and workshops. Her signature program for college students is called Project PreRich, and her signature program for the everyday adult is called A to Z Credit.

YOU ARE ENOUGH

You Are Enough To Make It Matter!
By Ryan C. Greene

"You have the power to set the expiration date on your failures. The moment you get back up, your failures become success stories."
Ryan C. Greene

There I was, working a job I hated. A job I felt was literally sucking the life out of me every single time I walked into the place. Each morning it was the same routine. I would sit in the parking lot and think of all the better ways I could be spending the next eight hours instead of being tied to that desk and phone. Eventually, I'd walk towards the employee entrance and up the stairs to the third floor. Then, I would look over the rail to the first floor below and ponder the same question, "If I jumped, would this fall kill me?"

To be clear, I wasn't suicidal. I would never kill myself. But that situation made me feel like I was committing suicide to my purpose, passions, and potential. Each day I questioned, "Is this going to be the day I get fed up and quit, or is this the day they are finally going to fire me?" I was stuck in a position where I knew I didn't matter. Yet, there I was, allowing it all to happen. Eventually, my employment ended. I declared that day that I would never again be that guy selling himself short for a check.

If you're going to live life, you might as well make it matter.

YOU ARE ENOUGH

That day I decided my sole purpose moving forward would be to create **unforgettable impact** and **abundant fulfillment** in my life and others. I had to make my life matter! I could no longer continue living life below the levels to which I was purposed to ascend. I decided that I was enough!

I want you to know that you are enough. Who you are, what you know, your experiences, your gifts, the value you bring is enough. You have everything you need to create a life of unforgettable impact on others while also being abundantly fulfilled by what you do.

I'm going to let you in on a little secret—your happiness matters. You do not have to serve others at the peril of your own joy. Stated differently, helping others shouldn't hurt you. I don't know when and how we started believing that, because your purpose may be aligned with service to others, that your own joy and happiness must then be forfeited for the good of those whom you serve. It's one thing to make sacrifices in service to others, but never should those sacrifices repay you in pain. One sacrifice you should never be willing to make is your fulfillment.

If you allow me, I want to help you create a life of unforgettable impact and fulfillment. I want to give you a free gift as my way of saying, "Thank you." Simply text the word MATTER to (614) 333-0338 to get instant access to a free download just for you.

You deserve to live life at its highest levels. You have everything within you already. YOU ARE ENOUGH! I look forward to helping you MAKE IT MATTER!

BIO:

Whether via a stage in front of thousands, over the radio and television airwaves, or through one of his many bestselling books, "The Passionpreneur," Ryan C. Greene serves as an Author Revenue Strategist for authors and speakers. Ryan is the author of ten books, hosts and executive produces several podcasts and web shows and is the founder of Indie Author PRO, specializing in teaching authors how to monetize their content, automate their business, and become top-revenue authors without being famous.

CONTACT:

Work with Ryan on your book or book him to speak:
www.ryancgreene.com

Follow Ryan on all social media and YouTube: @rygspeaks

YOU ARE ENOUGH

Message From Me-To-Me
By Christopher Hampton

*"I praise you because I am fearfully and wonderfully
made; your works are wonderful, I know that full
well."*
Psalm 139:14

Dear Me:

I am writing this message to you as a reminder. There will be times
when your vision seems blurry and on shaky ground. Challenges will
come along your journey, and obstacles will seem to block your
way. You will become discouraged and feel that for every step
forward, you take three steps backward. You will lose focus and begin
to wonder if the sacrifices made were even worth it. When those times
come, I want you to refer to this message and recollect who you are
and the gifts you bring to this world!

Remember two very important things. First of all, you are enough! I
know that when you look at your current situation that you are filled
with doubt. You are in seed form. A forest does not emerge
overnight. It begins its journey as a handful of seeds. The
resulting expansive forest develops over time and receives support
from its environment to produce life. It is the same with you. There is
a world waiting to be supported, encouraged, empowered, and
impacted by your gifts, talents, and abilities. Your perspective,
insightful solutions, and experiences are necessary for the growth of

others. You lack nothing because everything required for you to change lives resides within you. You are fully equipped for this life. Do not allow temporary circumstances to rob you and this world of your vision. Anything of value takes time to develop. You are not late. You are right on time. Every setback is adding credibility to your story. Keep pushing forward with the vision right in front of you. The mere fact that you can still see the vision is evidence that the vision is possible.

Do not allow frustrations, delays, or denials to derail your progress. I want you to acknowledge that any setback is a growth opportunity, and I hope you embrace each phase of your development. Realize that any time you are in transition, you are one step closer to fulfilling your vision. You are closer to becoming who you are called to be. Whenever doubt arises, just look back at all that you have accomplished thus far. No, you are not where you want to be, but you are closer than you were yesterday. Stop discounting your accomplishments. Celebrate your progress; just do not remain there. There is joy in the discovery that everything you need is truly inside of you.

Secondly, I want to remind you that you are unique. It is your uniqueness that qualifies you to pursue your vision. You will be tempted during your pursuit to settle and blend in with the crowd. Giving in would be a travesty and an insult to your vision. Do not change course when others do not accept your uniqueness. That is alright. The people you are meant to bless will recognize and value the treasure that you are.

Believe it and keep pursuing your vision!

Sincerely,

Me

BIO:

Christopher Hampton is the founder of the CHAMPIAM Organization. Chris enjoys challenging entrepreneurs, leaders, and youth organizations to break out of their comfort zones, empowering and equipping them to release their inner champ. Chris has been called a motivational teacher. He is sought after for his ability to present life-changing messages in an inspirational, empowering, and educational style. Chris challenges his audience to live their lives on purpose, pursue their passions, and live by vision and not by sight. Everyone has an inner champ. Chris is committed to helping you release the CHAMPIAM in you.

YOU ARE ENOUGH

Unlock Your Purpose: The World is Waiting on You!

By Rasheda Hatchett, MN, RN

"For I know the plans I have for you," declares the
Lord, plans to prosper you and not to harm you, plans
to give you hope and a future."
Jeremiah 29:11

I grew up in a house where ladies were to be quiet, poised, and polished, and I was born loud and on the move. I spent years feeling like I was too much; too much to handle, too loud, too outspoken, just simply too much. I did all I could to fit the mold of a lady, but I was longing just to be me. Not feeling perfect made me question myself, and I was convinced I lacked in every aspect of my life, and I yearned to be free to simply be myself, loud, proud, and full of passion. I tried to fill the void in my heart with education. I sought knowledge like a butterfly seeks flowers for nectar. I thought the only way for my voice to be heard was with the power of all the knowledge I gained behind it. What I didn't anticipate is never getting to the place of feeling enough. I found myself looking to the next accomplishment for validation, and each time, I was left with a longing for something more. After I attained my master's degree, it was no different. I had attained career success; I was in the upper 12% of my profession as a master's prepared nurse, and still, I felt I wasn't enough.

As I began my self-discovery and personal development journey, I was brought back to my first love, my passion, that thing that lit me on fire;

[167]

YOU ARE ENOUGH

SPEAKING to inspire and transform! I had been talking my whole life, but I wasn't speaking what was truly on my heart. I wasn't walking in my purpose. The thing about not living *your* purpose-driven life is, you'll always feel as if something is missing. I knew my calling was waiting on me, and as much as I tried to fill the void in my life with other things, it kept tugging at me. See, your passion will follow you. It may walk quietly beside you as you navigate your way through the journey of life, but it never leaves. It's always right there waiting for you to realize you have a job to do. I simply had to decide I was going to follow my purpose. I was put on this earth to inspire women to greatness and guide them through their own journey of self-discovery. My journey required me to realize I was enough for who I was truly meant to serve. They didn't want me perfect; they didn't want me polished. They wanted me just as I am flawed and ready to serve with my whole heart. When I made the shift and began to walk in the belief that I was enough, the world opened up to me, and I was able to see my own greatness. I began to show up in a way that attracted new opportunities. I was no longer chasing success because I believed by virtue of being, I was success personified!

BIO:

Author | Speaker | Resilience Strategist | Resilience Based Leadership Coach | Entrepreneur

Rasheda is the CEO of Rasheda Hatchett Media, LLC, a coaching and consulting firm steeped in her passion for women's leadership and wellness.

Rasheda is a three-time author, dynamic speaker, resilience strategist, and coach. Through her coaching and consulting firm, Rasheda is on a mission to coach female leaders from burnout and overwhelm to T.H.R.I.V.E. and confidently own their power. She is the creator of the "Audacity to T.H.R.I.V.E." coaching program designed for powerful visionaries desiring to beat burnout and expand.

YOU ARE ENOUGH

Finding Beauty in Your Brokenness
By Andrea Hayden

*"There is no perfection, only beautiful versions of
brokenness."*
Shannon L. Alder

In today's culture, life feels difficult at times - crushed by
commitments, by time, and by the self-inflicted weight of our own
expectations. Many of us are over-burdened with our unhealed
wounds, our tragic losses, and our shameful truths.

The inner despair remains intact, rendering us hopeless and sitting on
the sidelines of life. When the DIY quick fixes of confronting our
brokenness are no longer working, we may be tempted to hide the
scars in fear of rejection, shame, dislike, or disdain. If this sounds like
you, realize you are not alone!

We often feel it is too much work to dive into our pain and expect
progress to look like an upward slope. Often filled with ebbs and
flows, both are integral to the discovery process. To find the beauty in
our brokenness, we must start by embracing our imperfections, flaws
and own our authentic story.

Our stories are our broken pieces, and they may be vastly different, yet
the pain and shame feel the same. Even though your dreams may feel
shattered because of health issues, broken families, marriages, and

relationships, the good news is you are never too broken for restoration, never too shattered for repair and never beyond healing.

For years, I have felt I did not fit in. I did not realize until later in life that I had so many cracks, jagged edges and broken pieces created by the uncertainty during my foundational years from my mother passing away when I was only thirteen months old. I have experienced most of the listed broken areas during my life. Fortunately, I have the innate ability to always dream of better and I'm willing to do the work to reveal an amazing story about the true essence of resilience and strength.

I believe we are called to transform and look for any positive way to cope with traumatic events, learn from negative experiences, and take the best from it. Our testimony points straight to God and what He has done and continues to do in your life. He will take our mess and orchestrate it into a message that will bring comfort to others in their desperate time of need and darkness. ***Remember***; Our story is about us, but not for you!

A powerful metaphor for healing and hope is the ***Japanese art of kintsugi*** – the centuries old art of mending broken pottery, the art of precious scars, turning what is broken into beautiful, cherished pieces, by filling the cracks and crevices with lines of fine gold. Instead of hiding the flawed repairs, Kintsugi artists highlight them to make something beautiful out of brokenness, becoming more beautiful and valuable in the restoration process thanks to its "Scars." The message conveys how to see the beauty through the reinvention of ourselves.

I challenge you to work through your pain to identify your Purpose, Meaning, Healing, and Joy. My prayer is you find hope in knowing that whatever you are struggling through – ***You Are Enough***!

BIO:

Andrea Hayden, owner of The Hair Management Group, has 39 years in the Cosmetology and Trichology industry. Featured in Essence magazine, she was listed as one of seven hair loss experts in the country. As a visionary, Andrea has curated and directed global events and educational conferences all over the U.S.

Andrea has reinvented herself, bringing a wealth of entrepreneurial experience to her Business Consultant Agency. She is known as a change agent with an abundance mindset. Andrea is a trusted resource for women beauty professionals seeking profitable opportunities to maximize their gifts, while achieving life freedom.

YOU ARE ENOUGH

No Warranty... As-Is

By Gene E. Hayden, Jr.

"Yea, though I walk through the valley of the shadow
of death..."
Psalm 23:4 (NLT)

Imagine sitting in almost complete darkness. The only light protrudes from the hallway underneath the closed door. The only sound is my significant other's subtle breathing as she sleeps. Here is one of the few places where my plight is understood. Here, as the doctors tend to my wife, they also ask about my needs. It is something I have rarely thought about in the past, but it is a reality for many in my situation. When you care for someone with a chronic illness, much of the attention goes towards their needs, and for good reason. I am not referring to caring for someone thrust into a caregiving role. I am referring to getting involved with someone whose illness is "invisible." They live their life with a constant reality that something could go terribly wrong at any time. Being a caregiver for someone who does not look sick brings about its own challenges.

When I met my wife, the subject of chronic illness never came up in our everyday conversation. As our relationship grew, I started noticing little things. To provide some perspective, my wife has Lupus and Rheumatoid Arthritis. For most, when you meet her, you would never know. You see, my wife is beautiful, smart, vibrant, astute, and caring. These are the characteristics I fell in love with, but that does not mean I did not have reservations. Was there a true understanding of what I was about to get into? No! I am sure the same is true for many others. But what do you do when you are in it for the long haul? For me…it was understanding.

Understanding the illness does not mean you can handle any situation that may come up. It means that you make the necessary life changes to ensure a happy and vibrant relationship. For me, it was knowing that she was always going to be tired…just at different levels. In turn, I was also going to be tired trying to be superman. Look, we have all been there when caring for someone with chronic illness; we feel like we must do everything. In addition, you will have family and friends who will not understand the complexity of your relationship, and that is ok. For the men, you will doubt yourself. It is hard to see the person you love in constant pain. Admit helplessness and seek help. That means being vulnerable. I say all of this to state one simple fact. It is not easy living, loving, and caring for someone with a chronic disease, but it is worth it.

Despite the limitations that sometimes plague us, me and my wife have had great life experiences. We have traveled all over the world. She is a self-made entrepreneur with over thirty years in business. There is one aspect I am always reminded of when instances may not go as planned for our relationship. I got into this relationship with "No Warranty…As-Is," and I Love It!

BIO:

Gene Hayden guides members and their families to manage details of their varying accounts as a Survivor Relations representative to assist them after a loved one's death. He is a graduate of the United States Air Force Academy and was honorably retired after twenty years of service, finishing his career as a project manager for the U.S. Air Force's Sexual Assault Prevention and Response Team program. Gene loves to teach and is currently pursuing a master's in adult education. A devout husband, he has been married for over 22 years and parent to a little fur baby.

YOU ARE ENOUGH

Faith the Size of a Mustard Seed
By Phyllis Lenora Henry

"And Jesus said unto them, Because of your unbelief:
for verily I say unto you, If you have faith as a grain
of a mustard seed, Ye shall say unto this mountain,
Remove hence to yonder place, and it shall remove,
and nothing shall be impossible unto you."
Matthew 17:20 (KJV)

You are enough to overcome challenges, fears, and self-doubt. I overcame my challenges by perseverance and my faith in God. The definition of perseverance is a continued effort to do or achieve something despite difficulties, failure, or opposition. Perseverance is an important character trait for you to be successful in life. The keys of perseverance I used to focus on my goal include:

- Know where you are going and what you are trying to achieve,

- Have a strong mindset to WIN, and

- Continue to be persistent about sticking to your purpose.

In Philippians 4:13, it reads, "I can do all things through Christ which strengthens me." You are enough to thrive: Stay FOCUSED! Remember, "With God all things are possible." You have to press your way. You are enough to overcome your challenges. How did I persevere? I was determined to achieve my goal. I knew if I worked

[179]

hard and was determined to succeed through difficulties, I would persevere and succeed in any area of life.

Fear has a way of gripping us. You have to believe that you are enough to take the risk. God said He did not give us a spirit of fear but love, power, and a sound mind. I was afraid and didn't know if I would succeed, but I had to make a shift to win. The word of God carried me. Joshua 1:9, "Be strong and courageous, do not be frightened or dismayed God is with you wherever you go." Keep your faith and believe in the word of God.

How to keep your faith up? Pray to God and know that to whom much is given, much is required. When you have hope, you have faith. My faith gave me hope. God worked in my favor. Always feed your faith through the word of God. Trust God, pray every day, and read the scriptures. The Bible says, "ask anything in my Son's name and I will do it." I asked God for a place to work, and He provided! When you feel like giving up, remember these words: "Let us not grow weary of doing good for in due season we shall reap if we do not faint or give up." Call upon the name of the Lord when you are going through challenges. We often feel alone, and nobody understands, but God does. Look to the hills from which cometh your help; all of your help comes from the Lord. I have triumphed over the enemy, and he is in my rearview. Step into perseverance and activate your faith. That's why I am a successful Salon Owner of 25 years. Now, this is having Faith the size of a mustard seed.

BIO:

Phyllis Henry, CEO and Master Stylist of The Unique Touch Salon in Newark, Delaware, began her career in the beauty industry in 1982. In addition to the styling salon, she is also a licensed Cosmetology Instructor, a licensed minister, and an entrepreneur of Paparazzi Jewelry and Mary Kay Cosmetics.

Phyllis holds a Bachelor of Arts Degree from the Church of the Living Word School of Theology and School of Ministry. Phyllis acknowledges that to succeed in life, you must have faith the size of a mustard seed. Faith is the evidence.

To reach Phyllis, go to https://www.Instagram.com/jazzyladyphyllis https:/www.Facebook.com/Phyllis.Henry, and lenorahsisco@gmail.com

YOU ARE ENOUGH

Created by the Creator to be Enough!
By Donna Hicks Izzard

"I was created by the creator to be enough."
Donna Izzard

This little Black girl from Harlem, NY, the home of the historic Apollo Theater, makes a statement that I am enough. There are so many women with visions, dreams, and desires who have been stopped from being all that they were created to be because someone tells them that they are not enough. I am here to proclaim that being featured as a speaker with the legendary Master Motivator, Les Brown and

Dr. Cheryl Wood tells me that I am ENOUGH.

I, too, was a woman told that she did not have everything to be enough, and I started to believe that narrative for my life. These are examples of when I did not believe that I was enough:

Did not think I was enough growing up in Harlem.
Did not think I was enough in Corporate America to be an executive.
Did not think I was enough, always a bridesmaid and never a wife.
Did not think I was enough to be an author.
Did not think I was enough to be a Minister used by God.
Did not think I was enough around all of the Rev. Drs., Bishops, and Apostles in the Ministry.
Did not think I was enough to be a Business Owner.

YOU ARE ENOUGH

Did not think I was enough to be a Coach.
Did not think I was enough to be a mom.

BUT GOD!!!! God told me I was enough when He created me in His image. By accomplishing what I thought was impossible, my incredible journey has proven that I am enough. It was not an easy journey, but it was my journey to press forward to pour into another sister that she is enough.

Sister, I want to encourage you that you are enough. It's important that you make a decision today that you are enough. Give yourself permission to be enough. Do you find yourself asking yourself this question, "am I enough?" When you decide that "I am enough," it will be a pivotal moment in your life and will give you the opportunity to pursue purpose with an intention. It's your time to run your race of "I am enough" at your pace. Sis, stop looking to the left or the right and look ahead because you are enough. We often talk ourselves into foolishness by accepting the voice of the adversary that will whisper that you are not enough. I have also embraced the fact that I become what I speak; I am who I say I am. If I say I am enough, then I am enough. It's just that easy, Sis, speak your truth. The only thing it costs is the time that it takes for you to say it.

Lastly, when the "belief-killer" comes to attack your thoughts on believing that "I am enough," get back on track by asking yourself this question:
Who will you believe, God or the adversary?

BIO:

Author, International Speaker, Women Empowerment Leader, and Multiple Revenue Streams Strategist. Donna helps highly successful corporate professionals and faith-based leaders to blend their expertise and brilliance into profitable businesses while maintaining their full-time careers and ministries.

For several years, she was the business manager for a former "White House Ambassador." As a training and development professional in the legal industry with over 25 years of experience, she has mentored women to move up the corporate ladder. Donna was tagged as one of the top coaches to watch by Huffington Post and most recently recognized as one of the top 30 Black Global leaders by Impact Magazine.

YOU ARE ENOUGH

Pivot, Prepare And Lead With Confidence

By Dr. Karen Hills Pruden

"For I know the plans I have for you," declares the
Lord, "plans to prosper you and not to harm you,
plans to give you hope and a future."
Jeremiah 29:11

You are enough. There were times when hearing those words would have helped me push through adversity with fewer emotional scars. I grew up in a corporate structure where often I was the only person of color and sometimes the only woman. I felt lonely.

However, as I reflect, I know I have been blessed despite trials and tribulations. I was offered a job with a national employer two days after graduating with my master's degree. I was thrilled.

As a youngster, the adults in my life believed the more education I achieved, the better my life would be. I attained a terminal degree (doctorate). Only 1.68% of Americans have this accomplishment. This is the highest degree in education.

Those same adults failed to prepare me that some employees would not welcome my presence in the workplace. No matter how competent I was, no matter how educated I was, or how smart I was, I was not welcome. My melanin presence was a perceived threat to their status.

YOU ARE ENOUGH

One supervisor treated my every grammatical error as if it were a sin against God. It was hard not to notice the same scrutiny was not applied towards others.

With few leaders of my race or gender, there was no one in my workplace to encourage me to aspire to the next level in my career. I simply believed and listened to my inner voice whispering to me, "*You are enough, keep moving.*"

To figure out what my next career step should be, I read professional journals. I went to conferences. I hired a mentor from LinkedIn for $350 an hour who coached me monthly for an entire year. I researched on LinkedIn the education and credentials of those in my senior leadership positions. I copied their paths.

The *pivot* for me was to mentally disregard the non-verbal, passive-aggressive behaviors of those in the workplace towards me. As a human resource professional, I knew the protections that the laws afforded me. When the line was crossed (and it was), I asserted my rights.

I did not get sidetracked by the pettiness that challenged my existence in the workplace. I continued to collect credentials to be qualified when a promotion presented itself. And my opportunity came along with the hiring of an African American Vice President of Human Resources.

She was the first African American Human Resources Vice President. Within a year, most of the directors who reported to her left the company or retired. Ironically, this exodus paved the way for the next in line to move up. The second in the chain were African Americans. We were all promoted due to the sudden retirements.

The lesson here is, you must excel professionally despite adversity. When opportunity strikes, you must be qualified. I am now in the C-Suite as a Chief Human Resource Officer. That earlier promotion started my vertical trajectory towards the C-Suite.

YOU ARE ENOUGH! Prepare in spite of the objections of others.

BIO:

Dr. Karen Hills Pruden is the *Career Elevation Expert* for women seeking senior leadership positions. She has two decades of HR leadership experience, influencing employees through speaking, coaching, workshops, and ten book publications. She is a multipreneur global speaker. She works as a Chief Human Resource Officer/Assistant Vice President, the CEO of Pruden Global Business Solutions Consulting, and Founder of Sister Leaders Conference.

A graduate of Yale University Women's Leadership Program, she has been featured by Virginia SHRM, Society for Diversity, Black Wall Street, SpeakerCon, VCU, Global Fluency, EmpoweringHER, NAACP, and Peninsula Chamber of Commerce.

Website: https://www.sisterleadersconference.com

YOU ARE ENOUGH

Your Shine is Enough

By B. Jacqueline Jeter

"You may be the change and light needed by others,
to shine on their path."
Sunday Adelaja

One day as I was sitting reading one of my favorite books, everything went dark. No, the electricity did not go out, but the light bulb in my lamp did. I turned on the overhead light and went to find a bulb to replace it but unfortunately, to my chagrin, I didn't have the necessary 60-watt bulb I needed for that particular lamp.

Light in itself can affect the atmosphere and mood of a room. Light can be calming. In my bedroom and reading area, I have lamps that fit 60-watt bulbs. Light can be exciting and energetic. In my bathroom and kitchen, I have bulbs that are a higher wattage and energy. Light can provide direction and protection. Think about the amount of wattage necessary for a lighthouse or a motion sensor, or a spotlight.

You might say, why not just use another wattage bulb to put in my lamp? If I had put a 100-watt bulb in the lamp, it not only would have messed up my lamp or blown the bulb, it could have also caused an electrical issue in my house.

The next day, I found myself in the hardware store. As I lingered there looking at all the light bulbs, I saw different wattages, shapes, and sizes. Each bulb served a purpose. It was intentionally designed and created because of necessity.

While standing there, it hit me how much this aisle represented mankind. God designed us each for our respective purposes. He did not haphazardly create us but was intentional in our individual designs. He gave each of us our own wattage at which to show up and shine in this world for however long He deems. We each must know the wattage for which we were created to reflect. If I was created to be that 100-watt bulb but am trying to fit myself in 60-watt situations, I'm not only providing the incorrect illumination, I am putting myself and others at risk. The opposite is true. If I need the brightness of a 100-watt bulb but am only getting 60, then I don't have enough for my task at hand. In each circumstance, I am outside my purpose and no benefit to anyone.

My reading lamp was manufactured to handle 60 watts, and it was just enough for that lamp. Guess what? You, too, are enough for where and what you need to shine. You may be a 25-watt bulb, or 40-watt bulb, or 60 or a 100. You might be LED or incandescent. Your mere presence and the boldness with which you show up can alter the flow of a situation. The main thing to remember is that you have the necessity. You have validity, and your light is critical in this world. You are here because someone needs your level of illumination. So stop dimming your light and dimming your shine and Up Your Wattage™.

BIO:

A stone dropped in a lake creates ripples farther than the eye can see or one can feel. It causes a necessary disruption in the ecosystem. When it comes to transformation, B. Jacqueline Jeter is that stone.

Transformational Growth Strategist. CEO and Founder of Grow, Lead and Prosper™, which equips women to conquer limited mindsets personally, professionally, and spiritually.

Jacqueline holds several degrees and certificates, is a certified Vision Coach, a celebrated Independent Certified Leadership Coach, Teacher and Speaker with The John Maxwell Team, an ordained minister, and boasts a 28 plus year career as a consummate pharmaceutical development scientist.

YOU ARE ENOUGH

You Are Enough to Thrive After 40
By Ingrid Lamour-Thomas

*"Sometimes your only available transportation is a
leap of faith."*
Margaret Shepard

You are enough to thrive after forty. Yes, you are. Forty is not final.
All you must do is start. Start chasing your dreams. Take decisive
action. Make a plan. Align yourself with like-minded individuals. Start
now and do not look back. ACT NOW!

That dream that has lived on the inside of you, in your heart, in your
soul is still there. It is waiting to be manifested. If you don't take the
time to do that thing that's pulling at your heartstring, that thing that's
whispering, "I was made for more," "I have a purpose," you will
always feel a void. You will always wonder, what if? What if I did
take a leap of faith? What if I bet on myself? What if I took a chance?
Well, it's time to ACT NOW!

Like you, I am a "late bloomer." I went back to college at 34 years old.
I spent the next eight years in school and earned my associate degree
up to my master's degree at 42 years old. I took a leap of faith and
started chasing my dreams in my forties and became a motivational
speaker, 4x Amazon bestselling author, and Nonprofit founder. You
can do it too. It's not too late. You are not too old. You are enough.

[195]

YOU ARE ENOUGH

I know you feel afraid. Feel the fear and do it anyway. Do it scared, do it hesitating, but DO IT ANYWAY! Learn to hold fear in one hand, your passion, purpose, and destiny in the other, and go forward. Take action in the presence of fear. Brené Brown states, "Courage starts with showing up and letting ourselves be seen." Show up for yourself this time. Chase your dreams this time. Bet on yourself this time. Build your legacy this time. Go for it! You are enough to thrive after 40.

In conclusion, I want to share this famous Og Mandino quote which I love:

"I will act now. I will act now. I will act now. Henceforth, I will repeat these words each hour, each day, every day, until the words become as much a habit as my breathing, and the action which follows becomes as instinctive as the blinking of my eyelids. With these words, I can condition my mind to perform every action necessary for my success. I will act now. I will repeat these words again and again and again. I will walk where failures fear to walk. I will work when failures seek rest. I will act now, for now, is all I have. Tomorrow is the day reserved for the labor of the lazy. I am not lazy. Tomorrow is the day when failure will succeed. I am not a failure. I will act now. Success will not wait. If I delay, success will become wed to another and lost to me forever. This is the time. This is the place. I am the person."

Act now. Your legacy awaits… You matter. You are enough!

BIO:

Ingrid Lamour-Thomas is an international motivational speaker, 4x Amazon bestselling author, and the founder of The Green Light Movement, LLC. which empowers successful, professional career women approaching or over 40 who feel stuck, behind, and wondering about their purpose, that it's not too late to boldly chase their dreams.

As a Confidence Strategist and Image Consultant, she helps women become more confident by looking great on the outside while feeling great on the inside so they can show up bolder, put their best foot forward, and go after what they want while looking chic!

IG, FB & Clubhouse: @IngridMotivates

www.thegreenlightmovement.info

YOU ARE ENOUGH

You Are Enough To Take Your Financial Power Back

By Erica Lane

*"You must gain control over your money or the lack
of it will forever control you."*
Dave Ramsey

It's funny that society has convinced us to be educated enough to make great money, but only ivy league experts or Wall Street executives are equipped with the full repertoire of resources to be effective in money management. And therefore, we hand over our financial power to them. All the while, we are responsible for any mishaps and must live with the consequences of any mistakes they make. I've put blood, sweat, and tears into building businesses grossing $750k annually and have lost everything because someone else was mismanaging my money. I felt alone, broke and broken. However, due to that tragedy, I learned effective money management skills that changed my life forever. In that experience, I learned that you first must focus on your most important asset before you can focus on money. And no, I do not mean homes, cars, stocks, or bonds. I mean your mind. You must believe you have everything in you to own your financial power! It's time to show yourself you are more than capable of creating a successful life in your finances. Money isn't just for 'them' to master. It's something we all need to handle with the right grit and grace.

YOU ARE ENOUGH

It's time to manifest your dreams and elevate your money by first telling it what to do, also known as your budget. Yes, you must get control of your bills, debts, credit, savings, and income, but it's so much more than that. Control your budget, and you can control all of your money.

Tip: It takes a village to assist you in your money goals. Be vocal to your loved ones about what you want and ask for expert guidance. And I know that may be difficult (It was difficult for me as I was the all doing, don't need anyone type) ...... before I realized the power of manifestation, education, and investing in me! There is no shame in getting support, especially when you're about to take back your power and achieve your financial dreams. Capitalize on your strengths and leverage experts to educate you in the areas you need. Never be afraid to invest with an expert in what you want to do or what you need to do. You will come out feeling more powerful and better able to achieve your financial dreams when you ask the right people (the right questions) for guidance.

The key to gaining your power back is being true to your circumstances. Recognize where you are now and the vision for your money future. It's time to think about what money does for you and what level of power you want to achieve. You don't have to do it the way anyone else does it – you have to be realistic and find what works for you, the way that makes the most sense to you.

This is your time to realize your financial power. Remember, belief, manifestation, control, guidance, education, investing, authenticity, and vision = financial power. I believe in you!

BIO:

The Money Elevation Strategist has developed an exceptional money management approach, which enabled her to triple her income in three years. She is an Award-Winning Money Coach, Best Selling Author, International Speaker, and Conference Visionary. Her definition of success is to inspire women to change their money habits and, therefore, financial outcomes. Her clients develop the clarity and fearlessness to achieve their goals and tell the money story of their dreams on their terms. She specializes in empowering women to Build, Restore and Elevate their money!

Follow Erica on Facebook/Instagram/Linkedin @iAmEricaLane

Get her complementary strategies at thebudgetstrategies.com

Or visit iAmEricaLane.com

YOU ARE ENOUGH

You Are Enough To Attack And Overcome Your Distractions.

By Saymendy Lloyd

"I no longer question distractions that come my way;
for I have come to view disruptions in my life as a part
of my journey to an extensive path through which I am
made strong."
Quote By saymendy Lloyd©2012

The likelihood of a catastrophic outcome is often the result of unexpected distractions in our lives, yet, you are enough to attack and overcome distractions regardless of what method or vessel it arrives through.

According to the Oxford Dictionary, Distraction is defined as "a thing that prevents someone from giving full attention to something else." In life, distractions are no respecter of persons or situations. We will all face them at various points and times. How we choose to deal with them will determine whether the distraction can be used as a moment of growth or an unfortunate moment of great harm. Have you ever experienced one mess after the other? One piece of bad news after the other; one disaster after another or one loss after another? As soon as you handle one, the other appears. You are not alone; they are meant to distract you, leaving you an emotional wreck and taking impulsive actions. During this period, find an anchor, do not waver, and be not idle. If not dealt with head-on, it reduces situational mindfulness, disastrous outcomes, and spiritual decline.

[203]

YOU ARE ENOUGH

You are enough to attack, overcome and challenge your distractions. It matters not how strong or disciplined one might be; we all face distractions and obstacles in life. It is meant to redirect your attention from your focus point.

If you handle your distractions poorly, it can stop what you so desire and have worked so hard on. It can haze your vision, disrupt your environment, penetrate through friendships, disrupt family dynamics, and deplete the very substance of meaningful relationships while bringing you to a complete standstill.

When the distractions of life arise, you must remember that you are capable, and YES! you are enough to rise above it and attack it while staying focused on your goals and things you are working towards.

There are times you may have no one to turn to, no one to call, or the situation may be such that you trust no one to share it with. With or without support, there are five key steps that you should take when the distractions of life come your way.

1.   Recognize that it is a distraction no matter its appearance or status

2.   Build up your strength to stay focused on the goal ahead - remember your past distractions and look at how you survived through them.

3.   Take action and be proactive, not allowing yourself to be carried away by the feeling(s) that it may stir up in you.

4.   Stay connected, be solid, focused, and unmovable.

5.   When distraction leads to a dead end, turn to your Heavenly Navigator- pull over and chat with the Master; tap into your faith, depend and lean on the providence of the Holy Spirit; God will hear and aid you.

Equipped with these tools, you should be able to face any distractions that are sure to come your way. And remember, you are enough to attack and overcome your distractions.

BIO:

Neuro-Transformational Coach, Founder/CEO of Women's Wing, Activist, Community Builder, Servant Leader, Trainer, and a Philanthropist.

Believing there's no higher calling than strengthening the foundations of humanity, she uses her unique and masterful ability to transform the minds of the least, last and forgotten. Developing a healthy reputation for authenticity, her originality and humility motivate audiences, penetrating areas most coaches shy away from. Saymendy's territory of coaching expands through communities, streets, byways, and institutions without prejudice. With tools and strategies to bring out potential traps within clients' desires, her coaching techniques inspire thousands.

YOU ARE ENOUGH

You Are the Apple of God's Eye
By Dr. Nicole S. Mason

*"For this is what the Lord Almighty says: "After the
Glorious One has sent me against the nations that
have plundered you-for whoever touches you touches
the apple of His eye-""*
Zechariah 2:8 (NIV)

You, my dear friend, are a MASTERPIECE! You are indeed God's
greatest handiwork. When He made you, He knew exactly what He
was doing. He knew just how much pressure to apply in your life. Let
me stop right here for a second because I could hear you saying,
"Really, God allowed that kind of pressure in my life?" My immediate
response to you is, you are still here, so the pressure did not break you.
For all of us, life has many twists, turns, ups and downs, to say the
least. But the one thing that I am sure of is this: GOD LOVES YOU,
AND YOU ARE THE APPLE OF HIS EYE. And what that means is,
God sent you to this Earth with everything inside of you that you need
to not only survive but thrive. At some point in our lives, we must
change our perspective about the matters that happen to us, have
happened to us, and will happen to us that impact us in a negative
manner, or we perceive the matters negatively. The Bible is clear; all
things really do work together for our good and God's glory.

Listen, I will be the first to tell you that experiencing pain is not fun.
When my Mom suddenly passed away in November 2005, while I was
eight months pregnant, I was angry at God and wondered if He really
loved me. The answer was a resounding YES! The reality is we all

[207]

experience the loss of a loved one. None of us can change that aspect of life. However, we can control and change how we respond. We all are made in the image of God and have the strength of God on the inside of us. Genesis 1 reminds us that God was intentional about creating us in His image and likeness. We were not an afterthought! And it does not matter how you were conceived; YOU ARE SUPPOSED TO BE HERE! YOU HAVE A PURPOSE, AND YOU ARE THE APPLE OF GOD'S EYE! Genesis 2 reminds us that we did not become living beings until God breathed into us. God is as close to us as the breath that we breathe.

Understanding this important truth has emboldened me, given me greater clarity of who I am, and bolstered my confidence. Although my parents affirmed me and provided positive and powerful messaging about my value and worth, I know that everyone did not start with that kind of environment. None of these things in life is a surprise to God. We live in a fallen world, and He knew that we all would falter and fail, so He built inside of each of us a direct link to His love! This love note is the spark to your internal flicker that is designed to be an inferno – YOU ARE LOVED, YOU ARE ENOUGH, AND YOU ARE THE APPLE OF GOD'S EYE!

BIO:

Dr. Nicole S. Mason is an attorney, international best-selling author, coach, and speaker. She has been empowering women for the past 20 years and was recognized by Maryland Governor Larry Hogan for her work. She helps women to Show Up Great in their lives. Dr. Nicole was recognized with the Inaugural Faith-Based Speaker of the Year Award in 2019 at the Premier Conference for Speakers, Speaker Con. She is also an award-winning professional writer. Named one of the 50 Great Writers You Should Be Reading, she was recently showcased in the Chicken Soup for the Soul® Book Series.

YOU ARE ENOUGH

You Can Do It

By Jocelin T. McElderry, RN, BSN

"I can do all things through CHRIST who strengthens me."
Philippians 4:13 (NKJV)

When I started this Entrepreneurship journey, I had no idea what I was getting into or doing. There are still times now that I am still cloudy about what I am doing, but I have made a pact with myself that whatever door GOD opens, I will walk, limp, crawl, or skip through it if I must! I know that sounds crazy but isn't that what GOD desires for us, that we take the leap in blind obedience to HIS WORD?

By trade and calling, I am a Registered Nurse, so you can imagine the learning curve it has taken for me on this journey. I went from all the policies and procedures being written to having to figure it all out. However, I know that as long as I remain teachable, I can accomplish anything.

Never allow yourself to get stuck in the land of I can't! If it's been done before, I know you can do it as well. Never get stuck in the land of I don't know how! I have always heard that when the student is ready, the teacher will appear. Think of me as your teacher today. I want to help you change the way you speak and remind you of who you are. You are Amazing, Awesome, Powerful, and Chosen. All of these adjectives describe you. Whose report will you believe? You are the answer to someone's problem, the Ying to someone's Yang, and the voice that will help lead them out of their wilderness!

YOU ARE ENOUGH

So, I say to you now, take up your bed and walk. Walk away from the idea that I can't, I don't know how, and push past the negative self-talk to the land of, "I can do ALL things through CHRIST who gives me strength." With GOD in your corner, there is no way you could lose. Make the decision to stay focused on the prize and not so much on the journey. The journey is what perfects you for life with the prize. It is so worth it in the end.

If I can, I know that you can too!!! You have so much greatness inside of you. It is time to answer the call to those that need you!! Take the Leap, Shoot the Shot and Answer the Call! Someone is waiting on you to Show Up!!

BIO:

CEO of JTR Consulting, LLC, which houses the Finishers Touch Concierge (Day of Event Coordination) and The Connection Specialist Coaching/Mentoring.

Jocelin is also a Registered Nurse of 36 years. She has a passion for people and the plight of people. She was able to retire with 31 years of service in Community Health. In her coaching, she works with women in mid-life (45-64) to help them connect first with themselves, to be able to connect with other leaders to grow their confidence and businesses.

Overcome Fear – Achieve Your Purpose
By Dr. Theresa A. Moseley

"If you can't figure out your purpose, figure out your passion. For your passion will lead you right into your purpose."
Bishop T.D. Jakes

You are enough to overcome your fears, discover your passion and live in your purpose.

Have you ever feared being successful? Does fear drive your emotions daily? Have you lost a loved one and you crawled into the fetal position on the floor just crying and grieving? Have you let other people define who you are? If so, you are not living in your purpose. You are enough to discover your purpose and become successful. You are enough to use those emotions to heal your pain. You are enough to overcome that grief and go back to living in your purpose. You are enough to know that you are still here and your purpose is divine. I remember growing up and not being my authentic self. I was who everyone thought I should be. I also lived in fear. Fear of not being perfect. Fear of not making straight A's. Fear of not having perfect attendance. Fear of getting blamed for something I did not do and getting punished for it. It wasn't until I was almost 30 when my father passed away that I realized that I did not have to be perfect, and I did not have to fear anything but fear itself.

YOU ARE ENOUGH

On that day, I realized that I could use my gift, follow my passion, and live in my purpose. My father was my protector. When he passed away, I had to learn how to protect myself. It's ironic that the last day I saw him was the day I received my Bachelors' Degree from Georgia State University. I was the first child in my family to receive a college degree. He told me to go into the world and live in my purpose. "Don't be afraid to achieve greatness. You are great." Those words resonated with me from my father, a man with an 8th-grade education who had the wisdom of a sage. No one told me my dad was terminally ill, but my gift of intuition told me everything. My father died six months later from lung cancer. As I laid on the floor and grieved his death, a voice from within me said, "Get up! Go live your life. I'm still with you." From that day on, I followed my gift, which is my voice and intuition. I use my voice to sing, speak, and write.

I followed my passion for helping other students maximize their potential academically, socially, and emotionally. I also used my passion to fulfill my purpose to make the world a safer and better place to live by teaching love, compassion, and peace. I use my gift, passion, and purpose to help professionals discover who they are and how their passion is aligned with their purpose. Discover what your gift is. Know your passion. Live in your purpose. "Life is but a short road to our ultimate destiny. Make peace, have compassion, and learn to love before you get there."

BIO:

Dr. Theresa A Moseley is a US Army Veteran, a central office school administrator, and the owner and CEO of TAM Creating Ambassadors of Peace LLC. In 2014, she published her first novel, *The Fourth Child: Five Decades of Hope*. Dr. Moseley was a contributing author in two anthologies, *Women of Virtue Walking in Excellence* and *Step into Leadership Greatness*. Her second book is a love story, *Two Decades Apart*. She is a motivational speaker, coach, and educational consultant. She writes positive messages in her books about passion, purpose, and peace.

YOU ARE ENOUGH

Know Your Worth. NO Apologies.
By Carol T. Muleta

"Life never gives you what you deserve but what you decided."
Tara Fela-Durotoye

Parents often seek my help when they can't get their children to do what they want them to. When I dig deeper, I usually find a communication problem centering on one or both of these -- clarity and commitment. When parents don't speak clearly, they invite confusion, leaving lots of room for 'creative' interpretation. When parents aren't committed to the message, children sense this and dismiss it. There's no sense of urgency to compel action. My advice?

- Decide what you want and believe in it.

- Say what you mean.

- Communicate firmly and respectfully.

- And whatever you do, DON'T BLINK.

Many of us struggle to articulate what we want with conviction. This challenge can arise when you're communicating the value of what you do professionally. Sometimes, people just won't get it or pretend they don't because then they'd have to acknowledge your skills or expertise. When I was starting out, my partner and I delivered a workshop to positive reviews. When we cited the event hosts for using some of our language in their promotional materials without attribution, they claimed our words weren't "clever" or "unique." Fast-forward nine years, and we successfully trademarked our work.

Surprisingly, some people recognize the value of what you deliver but don't want to pay for it. While talking with a business owner recently about my programs, he became very interested and inquired about the price. I shared the price (discounted for him). He then suggested I apply for a grant to pay for *me* to serve *his* company! I think not. You deserve to be fairly compensated for your hard-earned skills and expertise. You can negotiate compensation, but never let someone make you 'hunt and gather' elsewhere for what *they* should be paying you to serve them.

Sometimes, you may even find that others don't think you deserve to be in a space at all. I recall showing up for a ceremony honoring myself and others who completed a certification program. When one participant saw me arrive, she immediately turned to a program leader to ask, well above a whisper, what the qualifications were to receive certification. Surely, she knew this as she had just completed the program. In addition, she had seen me put in the hours taking various classes that positioned me for certification. Somehow, she doubted I could earn this honor and validation in the same manner she did. I would later attain additional certifications and build a platform with the knowledge and experience I acquired.

As the saying goes, you can show some people better than you can tell them. Maybe you work with them. Better yet, let them read about what they missed after you make it BIG! When pitching yourself, go in STRONG and remember:

- You've invested in yourself.

- You have something others need.

- You change lives with what you know.

- You are worth it. No apologies.

"We are what we believe we are." – C.S. Lewis

BIO:

Carol Muleta is a Parenting Strategist and Consultant. She created The Parenting 411, a portal where she engages parents and awakens the JOY in their journey through workshops, webinars, and private consultations. She teaches parents to address challenging behavior, build strong family connections, and foster their children's success in academics and life. Carol was named 2019 DC Mother of the Year® by American Mothers, Inc. She hosts the Parenting 411 radio show and was named Radio Personality of the Year at SpeakerCon 2019. She is the author of Mother's Work: Pearls of Wisdom & Gems from My Journey.

YOU ARE ENOUGH

Triumph Over Trauma

By Emma Norfleet-Haley

"Trauma creates change you don't choose. Healing is about creating change you do choose."
Michelle Rosenthal

I would like to share how "MY WELLNESS FOR SELF WAS FOR SOMEBODY ELSE," specifically as it relates to "Triumph Over Trauma." So, join me on this short trip down memory lane before I share a roadmap to success on how to resolve trauma and live your best.

Imagine a small 5- or 6-year-old little girl (me) awakened from a sound sleep at 2:00 AM and then being pulled 2 ½ miles through a wooded area. Now the reason this little girl was dragged into the woods by her oldest brother was to protect her and others from a drunken, raging, alcoholic father. Despite being accustomed to awakening chaos, this night would be sketched and ingrained in my head forever. My father (AKA - Dr. Jekyll & Mr. Hyde), as I frequently use when describing my trauma, had escalated from physical and emotional trauma to an attempted sexual assault against my sister.

Fortunately for this older sister, my oldest brother took a stand and stopped this heinous and despicable sexual assault against her. In addition to witnessing the above, my drunken father then threatened to kill my brother. As the drunk stumbled toward the closet for the gun, my fierce brother gathered all 7 siblings and rushed us into the safety of the woods. However, entering the woods for safety was short-lived.

I vividly recall to this day the sound of bullets whisking past my head as the fierce brother momentarily kneeled down amidst the danger and said these comforting words "I got you, baby girl, it's gonna be okay." I then felt the firm clasp of my brother's hand squeezing mine and pulling me to safety. I remember the twigs and branches slamming across my face, chest, and legs in the woods. Given that there was no time to put shoes on, the ground stubbles and brows poked holes in the bottom of my tiny feet as my brother dragged me 2 ½ miles to safety. Safety at that time was the home of my maternal aunt.

So, if YOU are one with unresolved trauma, YOU had no choice; however, are YOU ready to choose Healing? The above question will forever fuel and drive my mission to assist individuals to cope with unresolved trauma to live his/her best life. **The roadmap to success** starts by removing the trauma mask of repression, denial, sadness, nightmares, and flashbacks. Unresolved trauma can lead to Posttraumatic Stress, Generalized Anxiety, and Major Depressive Disorders, to name a few. In closing, weekly Trauma-Focused Cognitive Behavioral Therapy will provide a safe and therapeutic space for you to **"REFLECT, REJECT AND RESET"** your mind. Haley's Mind of Care Services, LLC's staff offer quality mental health services to include the above evidence-based practice. Contact HMOCS, LLC via the website: www.hmocs.org or agency email: info@hmocs.org, Office#: (240) 429-5390: Cell (240) 423-4109 if you are ready to "TRIUMPH OVER TRAUMA."

BIO:

Emma Norfleet-Haley, PsyD., LCSW, LICSW, LCSW-C, CAMS I is the President/CEO of Haley's Mind of Services, LLC. She is a trained mental health trauma expert and Co-author in Dr. Cheryl Wood's upcoming "I Am A Victor" book released on April 13, 2021. She will be Co-Author in Les Brown and Dr. Cheryl Wood's upcoming "You Are Enough" book released in June of 2021. Emma Norfleet-Haley and staff provide evidenced-based psychotherapies to help clients "TRIUMPH OVER TRAUMA." She facilitates CEU training for clinicians needing licensure renewal. Contact her via agency website www.hmocs.org; work#:(240)429-5390 & email: info@hmocs.org. Media: @askmsemma & facebook.com/emma.norfleethaley.

YOU ARE ENOUGH

The Magic Pen
By Ene Obi

"You can't start the next chapter of your life if you
keep re-reading the last one."
Michael McMillian

Imagine you are given a beautiful pen that fits perfectly in your fingers and writes elegantly. You're told that beauty is not the only attribute of this fine pen; it is a magic pen, custom-made just for you. Whatever you write with this pen becomes real. Because of its magical powers, it has only one purpose; to write the story of your life from today onwards. Your job is to think about your life and take the story from here, creating the next chapter as you would like it to be.

What story would you write?

Think about your dreams for your life. Think about what stirs your spirit and excites your soul.

You have within you, the talent, gifts and abilities to realise your biggest dreams. You have infinite potential to be all that you were destined to become. That dream you have inside of you is one of greatness, alerting you to the possibilities of who you can be. It is the greatness within you begging to be released. It is your future asking you to bless the world with your talents and gifts, telling you that it is time to pull that dream out from within you, reminding you that anything and everything is possible in your life because you are an unrepeatable miracle.

Life is not a straight path, and sometimes we get caught up in the distractions and disruptions we encounter. Sometimes our blessings come brilliantly disguised as challenges and setbacks. We lose our balance, letting our circumstances, fears and doubts stop us from exploring the experiences and possibilities of life.

Have you ever talked yourself out of exploring new horizons, perhaps of reaching for a big dream? Have you ever told yourself that you are not good enough? I'd like to banish that thought and tell you that you are enough. You are special and you are unique. You are perfect, not *in spite of* your imperfections but *because* of your imperfections.

So, with the magic pen in your hand, what story would you write?

Would you write about your failures, past mistakes, and pains?
Would you keep nailing yourself down in chains?
Would you say, "I stumbled, I fell, beaten and broken,
Confused, lost, weary, and shaken.
I felt I was worthless, laden with defects,
Until a voice said, 'Your imperfections make you perfect.
You are unique with your scars and your bruises,
For without them, you couldn't fulfill your uses.
Your voice, your strength, your past are your powers,
That give you wings to share your story of conquer.'
A student of life, I wear the crown with glory,
Now with my pen, I get to write my own story."
By Ene Obi

The chapter you are currently in is not the end of your story; you have more greatness within you. Take the pen and start writing your next chapter. And as you do, allow your greatness to shine, knowing that You Are Enough.

BIO:

Ene Obi lives in London, UK, and for almost three decades, enjoyed a successful career at some of the most recognisable global corporate organisations, mostly in Human Resources.

Ene discovered her gift for inspiration and sharing powerful life lessons and wisdom. This led her to create Ziano Mindspa, where she combines her experience, story, and passion to help women who are ready to reconnect with their core, expand their vision of themselves and develop the full potential and possibilities of their lives.

Ene is a Les Brown Power Voice certified speaker and has shared his virtual stage on multiple occasions.

YOU ARE ENOUGH

Your Story Makes Heroes
By Suzanne Peters

"The truth about stories is, that's all we are."
Thomas King

Everyone loves stories. Myself included. But it wasn't until I decided to become a motivational speaker that I realized just how important my own stories were.

In one story, I was married to a controlling and abusive man who was full of pride. In another, my business failed, leaving me completely bankrupt. My worst is when I found myself broke, depressed, lonely, and just so tired. So tired that I decided to take my own life. But something in me just wouldn't let me give up. Like that moment in a story where the protagonist shouldn't be able to carry on, but something rises up inside of them – an inexplicable resilience that seems to defy reality. I never saw myself as a hero, but I now know that the protagonist doesn't have to save the world to be a hero. Sometimes saving themselves is already enough.

One of the best things about stories, though, is that we have the power to change them. There is nothing that can strip you of your authorship – a fact that life has proven time and time again. Today, my story is being happily married, owning my own beautiful home, and my dream business, and I'm not done yet. For as long as we still have breath in our bodies, we are still writing our story. I know none of this would have been possible had it not been for mine.

YOU ARE ENOUGH

Today, I share my stories proudly because although they are about me, I know they are not for me. And yours are not just for you either. I implore you to embrace your stories, apply the lessons you learned, but also use your stories as a beacon for others. Your stories are more powerful than you know. Through action, a person becomes a hero, but through storytelling, that hero becomes a legend. And it sometimes takes hearing a legend for a person to take action.

It's up to you to perpetuate this cycle.

Your story can be the reason someone decides not to take their own life. Or the reason someone takes a second look in the mirror and says, "I am beautiful." Your story can make heroes out of ordinary people. But only of the people who hear it.

I don't believe we live in a perfect world. But I do believe we serve a perfect God, and although you may have been through a lot and your stories may be punctuated with pain, they were not in vain. They are penned for a purpose. God is the "author and perfecter of our faith," which means we are co-authors in our story. If your story has not reached something good, then it isn't finished yet. If it has, then it is time for it to reach others.

BIO:

Suzanne Peters is a women's empowerment coach, motivational speaker, author of the book Woman To Woman – How To Create The Life You Want, and host of the Woman To Woman Conversations Podcast.

Having transformed her own life, Suzanne uses her experiences and lessons learned to empower women and audiences worldwide to get clear on what they want and make it their reality.

Suzanne is also the CEO and Founder of Woman To Woman International Network Inc., a 501 C (3) non-profit organization that supports the personal and business development of women through grants.

YOU ARE ENOUGH

Keep Your Temple Healthy, Stop Filling It With C.R.A.P.!
By Tanya Y. Pritchett, PMP

"Do you not know that your body is a temple...?"
1 Corinthians 6:19

"Keeping your body healthy is an expression of gratitude..."
Thich Nhat Han

When attending church as a child, it was an act of reverence, as well as an expression of gratitude for all He's provided, to enter God's temple dressed in our best attire. I can imagine the reaction had we arrived and found the church filled with garbage - Outrage! "Who would do this? This lovely building wasn't constructed to hold garbage!"

Our bodily temple wasn't constructed to hold garbage either, yet we are quick to fill it with C.R.A.P. (calorie-rich and processed foods) like:

- **C**hemicals and carbonated sodas
- **R**efined sugars and flours
- **A**rtificial sweeteners and colorings
- **P**rocessed foods and preservatives

Then, we expect to use it for all the things it is constructed for, i.e., running around with the kids, sexual intimacy, and working in our chosen careers. It's hard to do those things when we're filled with the C.R.A.P. because it creates inflammation which can lead to fatigue, brain fog, low libido, chronic disease, etc.

Jim Rohn says, "Take care of your body; it's the only place you have to live." Taking care of our bodies is showing gratitude by keeping them healthy. We cover the outside of our temples with our best clothes to show respect and gratitude when entering a building, but then we fill our insides with garbage. Why? Often, it's because of a negative mindset and feeling like, "I'm not enough."

I was "skinny" growing up; the only shape I had was my ample backside which, these days, most would consider a gift. But I wasn't exposed to beautiful, curvy women like Beyonce' to help me feel like I was enough having those curves. I was teased by the girls in my school and didn't have gratitude for the shape I was given. It wasn't until years later when I developed a positive mindset that I knew I was enough.

I don't want you to have to wait years to know that "You Are Enough" no matter where you are on your health journey; allow me to share three things to help you clear the garbage from your temple:

1. **Mental Diet**- If we feed our minds with negative thoughts like, "I'm fat" or "I can't lose weight," then we start to believe it. We cannot hold two thoughts at the same time, so the next time you have a negative thought, **immediately** replace that thought with a positive one.

2. **Gratitude Journal**- Be intentional to boost your positive mindset. List at least 3-5 things you are grateful for each day and have at least one thing be related to your body, weight or health.

3. **Eat Healthy**- Start by adding two additional whole fruits and veggies to your daily intake, but Hosea 4:6 says, *"My people are destroyed for lack of knowledge…"* Therefore, seek the knowledge of what healthy eating means for YOU because you are unique and healthy eating is not a cookie-cutter process. Research or seek the support of a health coach.

Love yourself enough to live a healthy lifestyle because **You Are Enough!**

BIO:

Tanya believes, *"The best project to manage is one's own health."* After conquering her weight challenges, she formed TYPS4Life, LLC to coach busy professionals to do the same. Through attentiveness, knowledge, and experiences, she *creates* convenient plans that allow YOU to *release* weight and *increase* vitality and confidence to do what YOU *love* without spending hours in the gym or kitchen!

Tanya has a Master Nutrition Consultant Certificate from AFPA, is a PMP, and holds Bachelor's and Master's degrees in engineering and telecommunications. Her activities include Toastmasters, dance, photography, travel, and time with friends and family.

Connect via:

https://linktr.ee/typs4life

typs4life@gmail.com

YOU ARE ENOUGH

You Are Enough as God Intended…
By Debbie T. Proctor-Caldwell

*"**Great minds** discuss ideas; average **minds** discuss events; small **minds** discuss people."*
The words are attributed to social activist and former First Lady
Eleanor Roosevelt

You are ENOUGH with the complexion you have! Light, medium or dark can not look any better than it does on you!

You are ENOUGH with the hair that you have. It does not have to look like the latest trend or have a different texture than it currently has! The grey that is growing unruly and unmanageable is designed to represent the wisdom you gained through the struggles you have overcome. Let the silver shine; not many people understand the bragging rights that come with age.

You are ENOUGH with whatever disability, sickness, or ailment you have. You will show people how you can still do what you were meant to do in life, even through these walls.

You are ENOUGH to be successful even though you don't have a high school diploma, a college degree, or several degrees. One day you will walk among Kings and Queens, and Royalty and your presence will be demanded by millions due to your wisdom and intellect that no degree could capture.

YOU ARE ENOUGH

You are ENOUGH if you were raped, molested, abused, abandoned, and trashed. Your glory is not with people on Earth but with God in Heaven. People are not able to see your worth with their bare eyes.

You are ENOUGH if you were unloved, cheated on, ridiculed, made fun of, and hated. God loves you, and when envious people see that you are loved, they respond with anger, violence, and hate because they want to be you!

You are ENOUGH if you are a reader, into the arts, paint, or theatre. The world needs your paintbrush to continually paint a better world than the one we live in. Your ability to see what the world doesn't see is rare, and only you have it!

You are ENOUGH if you are an introvert, extrovert, tomboy, girlie girl, heterosexual, homosexual, bisexual, straight, transgender, female, male, or undefined. We see you, and you do not need titles to define you!

You are ENOUGH if no one believed in you, sang your praises, showered you with attention, or noticed you. You are noticed without you even knowing it. You have an aura that is so bright that it is blinding; it comes from within and can never go out like an eternal flame. You attract people to you like a magnet and create an ambiance for others that is addictive. You are what makes the difference in other people's day!

You are ENOUGH as you are to become what you were destined to be. You are not your past but the beginning of something special EVERY DAY. EVERY DAY is a new day to become a better YOU!

You are ENOUGH because no one can do you, like YOU! All of your struggles would have caused most to crumble. You shrugged your shoulder and flicked off the pain, worry, and hurt like it was a gnat. Why? Because you know what it means to be fearlessly and wonderfully made by GOD!

BIO:

Debbie Proctor-Caldwell is a Wife, Mother of two adult children and Stepmother to her bonus Son. She is from Southern Maryland but currently living in Washington D.C. In 2015, she retired as a police lieutenant from the United States Capitol Police in Washington D.C. with over 25 years of experience in law enforcement, investigations and public speaking and is now an author and an aspiring international motivational speaker. Debbie is a child of God and attends the First Baptist Church of Glen Arden of Maryland. She earned her Bachelor's and Masters of Science in Management from Johns Hopkins University of Baltimore, Maryland. Debbie is currently in the process of building her business that will serve to empower Women in leadership positions with the tools needed to have their voices heard to become successful leaders.

Email: TerenaCspeaks@gmail.com

Instagram: instagram.com/terenacspeaks

LinkedIn: Debbie Proctor-Caldwell, M.S.

YOU ARE ENOUGH

Self-Care Is Not A Beauty Regimen
By Tykesha Reed

"Come to me, all of you who are weary and burdened,
and I will give you rest."
Matthew 11:28 (NIV)

We are busy working. Some of us have stressful jobs, and we are often taking care of everyone… our children, spouse, or significant other, caregiving for family, and even being there for our friends. In our weariness, we often forget, feel guilty about taking the time, or simply do not schedule a time to care for ourselves with the same intentionality that we give others.

It is remarkable to be available for others, but we must also take time for ourselves. Perhaps you do take time for yourself; if so, that is awesome. However, I am optimistic that this message can still benefit you in some way. This message is for everyone! I hope you will have a clear mind to receive all that God is allowing me to pour into you because you are more than enough and deserve rest, as the scripture says. I will discuss the importance of being intentional with self-care and self-love.

Think about this; you spend numerous hours each week taking care of others. How many hours a week do you dedicate to yourself? It is essential to your mental health and well-being that you intentionally schedule "me time" or self-care time. We are not here to live a life of suffering. You deserve to be happy and to do things for yourself. Self-

[241]

care is not selfish! You can help others, but you must also help yourself. You cannot live a healthy, happy life by putting everyone else's needs in front of yours.

Love yourself and make yourself a priority. You are enough to prioritize self-care intentionally. You owe it to yourself! I challenge you to invest in your well-being each week, and I promise you will begin to feel less stressed and more fulfilled. Let's talk about self-care.

SELF-CARE IS NOT A BEAUTY REGIMEN! I am on a personal crusade to help people understand this. Self-care is you investing in yourself, period. The way that you invest in yourself is totally up to you. You can do pampering and external self-care, but more importantly, it should be about your whole existence; mind, body, and soul. Your mental health is at stake when you are constantly going and doing for others, and never rejuvenate yourself. You are worth scheduling self-care and sticking to it. Your life depends on it. Let's be intentional and explore some self-care strategies:

- Utilize a schedule
- Learn to say "No"
- Relax and disconnect
- Exercise regularly
- Find a hobby
- Read a book

Above is a short list of options that can get you started with a self-care routine. Just remember that you cannot take care of others if you are not well. Your family and friends need you to practice self-care and self-love. Love yourself enough to invest in your self-care so that you can live a healthy life.

SELF-CARE IS NOT OPTIONAL! You are worth investing in yourself.

Be blessed!

BIO:

Tykesha Reed is a Motivational Speaker and Coach. Her passion drives her to empower women and girls to be their best selves. As a motivational speaker, Tykesha teaches women how to achieve their goals and lead with intention. She focuses on leadership, self-improvement, and self-care.

Tykesha is a noteworthy leader and has been honored with the Technology Rising Star Award from the Women of Color STEM Conference and IBM Corporation. She is currently a doctoral candidate at Drexel University in Educational Leadership and Management. Tykesha's goal is to empower women and girls internationally.

Contact: theselfcareadvocate4u@gmail.com

Website: www.theselfcareadvocate4u.com

YOU ARE ENOUGH

Right to Thrive
By Nikki Rogers

"I will not die an unlived life.
I will not live in fear
of falling or catching fire."
Dawna Markova

Whether you're eight or 88 years old – courage, confidence, and curiosity will help you thrive in life. These three traits have repeatedly surfaced in my life as the keys to success.

Recently, my family participated in a workshop to create a family statement. As we worked through the exercises, we identified our core values, developed a motto, and documented our family mission statement. I observed my 8-year-old's high-level engagement with a mixture of surprise and pride. At such a young age, he was extremely clear about the values that mattered to him and easily articulated the areas in which he thought we as a family could improve. I was amazed as he took the lead in writing on our flipchart and sticky notes, contributed to the discussion, and expressed his point of view. He asked questions when there were terms, like "motto," that he didn't understand.

I marveled at my child's youthful exuberance for this strategic thinking exercise and his display of courage, confidence, and curiosity, and I was reminded of another relative - my great grandmother, Mary Burden. Born in 1899 in rural North Carolina, Grandma Mary was

[245]

functionally illiterate. Yet, she employed her innate intelligence to manage her finances, purchase her own home, and raise children who excelled in school. As a child, I thought she was smart, accomplished, and independent. As an adult, I can now appreciate the courage and confidence required to thrive as an elderly Black woman in a mostly segregated small town.

My child and my grandmother shared the reality of limited formal education and relatively narrow life experiences, and an ability to strategically navigate their respective challenges – both in theory and in practice. Although born more than a century apart, they both demonstrated an uncanny ability to succeed and inspire with their God-given abilities.

These two examples remind me that we are born with everything that we need to thrive – the courage to take on new challenges, confidence to know we will succeed, and curiosity about the world around us. The addition of skills, education, and professional and personal experience can impact our natural ability to thrive. How, as adults, do we remember, claim, and leverage these innate gifts?

We can channel these gifts through intentional reverence and implementation within our busy lives. After many years of risk-avoidance and living within societal expectations of success, I'm using my gifts to thrive on my own terms. I am now on a mission to cultivate the **courage** to explore new paths, engage new people and embody new ways of being necessary to seek what feeds my soul. I work daily on developing the **confidence** to claim joy as my birthright, inherited by virtue of the sacrifice and resilience of my ancestors. And lastly, I feed my **curiosity** by pursuing the knowledge that supports these efforts and other goals. I invite you to embark on a similar journey in your life and reclaim your right to thrive.

BIO:

Nikki A. Rogers is a strategist and transformation coach who believes life is too short not to do what you love. She is passionate about helping entrepreneurs build sustainable companies and supports business leaders in developing the mindset, strategy, and connections to create thriving businesses and build legacy wealth.

Nikki is the CEO of The Bladen Group, host of the Women Thriving in Business podcast, and an alumna of North Carolina A&T State University and UNC-Chapel Hill. You can connect with Nikki via www.bladen-group.com, LinkedIn: **linkedin.com/in/nikki-rogers,** and Instagram: @NikkiRogersOfficial.

YOU ARE ENOUGH

You Are Enough to be Broken and Beautiful

By Jacqueline Shaulis

"Sometimes things have to fall apart into place. But, I owe it to myself to be focused, consistent, and disciplined. My broken pieces are creating a beautiful masterpiece."
Jacqueline Shaulis, *Embrace Your Awesome*

<u>Vulnerability is the connector of one soul to another.</u>
Many people are afraid to show who they really are because they fear they will be destroyed. I call it *Clark Kent syndrome* – you have to calm down, button up, dumb down, and dullify yourself, so no one will know just how amazing you are. You have to pretend to be like the other humans and experience things like them rather than admit you are able to rise above it, so you're not busted.

Well, the jig is up. You cannot truly connect and speak authentically when you have barriers and falsehoods within you. *We feel it,* and no matter how much we like you, we won't fully believe in you or your message. Why should I trust you when you can't even be honest with yourself?

<u>Are you willing to stumble or springboard?</u>
I've discovered one of the biggest reasons people are thwarted in their growth is from clinging to the past in the hopes of understanding it. The sense of "I can't move on until I understand why this happened" can pervade your perspective and impede your progress.

[249]

YOU ARE ENOUGH

Christie Marie Sheldon has a great description of this phenomenon: "as long as you try to understand it, you are standing under it, and it hangs over you. Instead of trying to understand it, you should get over it so you can be free from it and walk away."

In other words, understanding can be a well-intentioned anchor dragging you to the bottom of the sea of regret. The "why" of your crummy situation is, frankly, irrelevant because even if you know *why*, you cannot change or remove the experience. But you can (and must) surpass it. It's your responsibility to move beyond it.

Allow yourself to be as amazing as you dreamed.
It all comes down to a choice. You can be as AWESOME as you allow yourself to be. You are amazing – that's a fact. Despite the billions of people on this planet, there is no one with the same blend of experiences, skills, quirks, talents, and abilities as you. The truth is that you are one of a kind and that alone is awesome.

When you are true to yourself and all that you have to offer, there's no room for errors because *you* fill the space. Oscar Wilde once said, "it's better to be an imperfect original than a perfect imitation." How true. When you are honest about your greatness and your shortcomings, people can relate to you, which leads to liking you, then trusting you, then buying into you.

Positive outlook draws good things to you.
Optimism breeds opportunity. The more positivity you bring to the table, the more you draw people to you and your solutions. When you think well of yourself, you energetically share that optimism and cause the perception of others to be stacked in your favor. How awesome is that? Very awesome – just like you!

BIO:

As "The Excitable Introvert," Jacqueline Shaulis guides introverted women of color to get seen, heard, and respected by embracing their AWESOME! Her 30+ years of communication and personal leadership experience grew from a challenging upbringing to an international speaker and 3-time bestselling author globally. She's shared her "Embrace your AWESOME" message on stages in nearly 20 countries for Fortune 500 corporations, notable organizations, and educational institutions and has been featured in numerous media outlets, including *Forbes, Doctor Oz, Romper, MarketWatch,* and *NerdWallet.*

YOU ARE ENOUGH

You Are Enough to Live a Purposeful Life

By Dr. Onika L. Shirley

"He who has a why to live can bear almost any how."
Friedrich Nietzsche

God doesn't call people who are qualified. He calls people who are willing, and He qualifies them, Philippians 1:1-2. As I think about being enough, I think about how we are uniquely and wonderfully made. When we cease to stand out, we begin to blend in. When the thoughts and values of the world concerning our bodies, our businesses, and our bank accounts begin to influence our minds, it takes hold of our emotions, behaviors, and attitudes. The world has tried to influence the life and purpose of each of us rather than the other way around. Purpose gives way to the world's identity, and it's time that we remember what our purpose is. It's time that we stand out because we were designed to be different.

This is not a season to just go with the flow, but it's time that we recognize who we are or seek to become aware of our purpose for being if we don't already know it. We have a purpose as a people and a nation, and we must avoid compromising who we are while remembering who we were born to be. Some people run on autopilot, allowing the automatic programs to play in their subconscious, not allowing themselves to see who they really are. We are sometimes raised in environments where dysfunction becomes our foundation, and we find ourselves doing what we think we need to do to get what

[253]

we desire. Sometimes our purpose is placed on pause to simply fit in where we don't belong. The truth is we need to trust ourselves and not be motivated by the hype of the world to simply fit in. It's time we have a deep, thoughtful, and sincere conversation with ourselves as to who we are and why we are here. This conversation must be intentional. You were born on purpose and for a purpose, and with nothing needing to be added, YOU ARE ENOUGH.

After the world experienced a pandemic, losing loved ones and friends, being locked down, and required to practice social distancing, many were tempted to believe they had no purpose. Some of our youth were tempted to give up on living the meaningful and purposeful life that Christ has called us to live. We don't have to give in to a world that encourages us to simply go with the flow. You are here for a reason, you have a place in this world, and you have work to do. Your work is unique to you, and it may not resemble the work of anyone you can compare to, and that's okay. You were created and called to maintain an exceptional focus and vision. You are called to the power of purpose. Purposeful living in the real world, we quickly realize that it's not always fair, but we learn to live by faith and not by sight. Remember, YOU ARE ENOUGH to live a purposeful life.

BIO:

Dr. Onika L. Shirley's mission is to serve God and the women of His kingdom by helping strong, powerful, and compassionate women harness their full potential and utilize their God-given gifts. Dr. O understands that every woman is unique, and one size simply does not fit all. She knows how to get people motivated and inspired. As a Christian counselor, she is not scared to walk with a client headfirst into the hurts, habits, and hang-ups, holding them back with her knowledge as a Christian counselor and her personal experiences as a Christian woman who survived life-altering challenges.

YOU ARE ENOUGH

You Are Enough to Build Your Empire
By Dr. Carlisa M. Smith

*"But thou shalt remember the Lord thy God: for it is
he that giveth thee the power to get wealth, that he
may establish his covenant which he sware unto thy
fathers, as it is this day."*
Deuteronomy 8:18

Fear is the false evidence about reality. I believe that everything we
want is on the opposite side of fear. You know you can do all things
through Christ that strengthens you. Visualize everything you desire.
Shoot for the stars and dream big! Now ask, believe, do your part, and
receive. Remember, faith without works is dead.

Now that you have had time to visualize, What is your dream career?
How much income do you desire? What do you want to invest in?
Where do you plan to vacation? Keep all the things that you desire in
front of you. Keep the result in mind personally, physically, and
professionally. As you build your empire, know that these key areas
are extremely important.

I was a child that grew up in government housing, a daughter of a
teenage mother. I witnessed domestic violence. I was a stressed-out
child and teenager. I got married, then divorced about eleven years
later, became a single mother, and had to start all over, but with two
children. Although I went through very challenging times, I was still
able to get back up and succeed despite the people hoping that I would

[257]

fail. I'm a witness that if life knocks you on your face, you can get back up and build your empire. I know if I was able to succeed, I know you can do it too.

My career of choice to build my empire is real estate. I began my career as a realtor. After being in the industry for several years, I became a real estate investor and purchased multiple properties. I love what I do. Currently, I am still purchasing, rehabbing, selling some, holding on to some of the properties, and building generational wealth. According to Andrew Carnegie, "Ninety percent of all millionaires became so through owning real estate."

There are multiple ways that you can utilize real estate to build your empire. You can be a property locator, wholesaler, rehabber, and seller. You can use the B.R.R.R.R formula; buy, rehab, rent, refi, and repeat. With this formula, you can hold on to your properties and build your multi-million-dollar portfolio.

Several tips to help you build your empire: Avoid negative and depressing conversations, eliminate time wasters in your life, maintain a winner's mentality, provide a solution to your customers' needs, focus on your opportunities, dominate your local area, and expand globally.

What you focus on will grow, so focus on what you want. Your integrity will always be remembered longer than your product. Honesty and integrity are priceless. Anyone who does business with you wants the truth. Liars are eventually exposed. Give people what they can't find anywhere else, and they will keep coming back. Take care of yourself; get proper rest. A rested mind makes good decisions.

Remember: "Some succeed because they are destined to, but most succeed because they are DETERMINED to." -Henry Van Dyke

BIO:

Dr. Carlisa M. Smith is a prominent generational wealth builder and an influential professional with over 27 years of proven experience. She is a highly sought-after speaker that is known to Educate, Inspire and Empower… Dr. Smith is the CEO of multiple organizations and holds several designations and affiliations. Dr. Smith is an established leader and educator committed to teaching others how to build an empire and implement life skills that contribute to her clients living their best lives now.

Mother | Best-Selling Author | Entrepreneur | International Speaker | Real Estate Empire Builder | Life Coach | Philanthropist | 561-688-1316 | drcarlisa.com | info@drcarlisa.com

YOU ARE ENOUGH

Walk in Confidence

By CoWano Ms Coco Stanley

"Confidence is one of the Keys to opening doors you are seeking."
CoWano Ms Coco Stanley

You are enough to walk in confidence, just believe it. Do you know you are born with confidence? You may believe that you don't have confidence in yourself because of some life experiences or you failed in something or didn't get that promotion you wanted. Maybe you don't have confidence because you grew up in a negative environment. The positive acts and behavior weren't there in your surroundings. You may feel like you don't have confidence because someone always threw limiting beliefs your way and you started believing it or you were told that you aren't good enough. Whatever the case may be, let me be the first to tell you that YOU ARE ENOUGH because God says you are. God's word in Psalms 139:14 says, "I am fearfully and wonderfully made: marvelous are thy works and that my soul knoweth right well." So, you are enough.

See let me tell you about myself. There have been times in my life where my confidence was lost, and I didn't believe in myself. In my high school days not getting accepting by those I felt like I wanted to fit in with made me lose confidence in myself. By the time my son was 10 and I was in my thirties, I had experienced 3 abusive relationships. Going through those relationships had me believing that I was not enough. I had developed low self-esteem as well as looking for validation from others. My underachievement came about because of my confidence within myself. Once I became aware of the loss of confidence within myself, I started to take action.

To have confidence is a daily task that must be done. Many things will come in every day that will creep in and try to steal that confidence that you have. So, it is up to you to get you in a place of having confidence in all areas of your life, such as career, business, personal, spiritual, financial, and mental. There are plenty of things that you can do like I did if you have lost your confidence. The main thing you should do is Meditate and Pray. Meditate and pray allows you to tap into your mind, body, and soul. It also allows you to release all energy within that does not belong. Again, you are unique and special in your own way. Another thing to do to get your confidence back is to start writing and speaking affirmation. Affirmations are just as important to do every day even if it doesn't feel real. Affirmations will help you become aware of your thoughts and words and limit negative thoughts. It helps you to surround yourself with positive people and things. Affirmation will help you believe in yourself and encourage yourself more. When building your confidence, it's good to read encouraging and motivating books. If you don't like reading, then find that book as audio to listen to it. If you need to build your confidence back NOW is the time.

BIO:

CoWano Ms Coco Stanley grew up in Minneapolis, MN. She now lives in Las Vegas, Nevada. One of the most significant events in her life was the birth of her son. She completed two master's degrees while raising her son. In the midst of the tough times she went through, she experienced a lack of confidence within herself due to several abusive relationships. She learned how to overcome a crisis of confidence & regained her confidence. CoWano's mission is to provide women with support & tools to overcome a crisis of confidence, to a path of starting their most successful business.

YOU ARE ENOUGH

Disappointment to Purpose

By Angelecia Stewart

*"Let the words of my mouth, and the meditation of my
heart be acceptable in thy sight, O LORD, my strength
and my redeemer."*
Psalm 19:14

I remember so many moments in my life when I felt I had no one to talk to, call on, or go to when I felt my lowest. I grew up without a mother and father, so I had to learn how to get up on my own every time I started to bend. I made so many mistakes because of the trauma I endured for so many years. I did not know what love, peace, and happiness meant.

But what is true is that when you are sick of being tired and miserable, walking around feeling like dry bones, you will become more self-aware of who you are and begin to make changes that will positively impact your life and surroundings.

I finally realized that I have the power to change what I wanted to become in life. I have the power to turn all the negative decisions in my past into positive ones in my present. I have the power to surround myself with like-minded individuals who make choices to do better because they want better in life. I have the power to walk in my purpose.

YOU ARE ENOUGH

God showed me how man can take anything away from me that was never in their possession to give me in the first place. So I chose to be happy. I chose to love myself. I chose to be at peace. I chose to care for myself first. Once I found myself, there isn't a day that goes by that I don't speak over my life what I desire for God to do for me.

I once had no confidence and no self-esteem in myself. I once did not know my name. I once did not know my own identity. I once did not know whether I was coming or going daily. But one thing I never lost sight of is that I have always had a friend in God. Although I didn't have my biological father in my life, God never left me, nor did He forsake me. Once God brought me out of the wilderness, I haven't looked back, and I've been running as His vessel ever since.

Speak life into your every circumstance, no matter the good or bad. Rebuke everything that attempts to hinder you from walking in your victory.

BIO:

I am an inspirational speaker, author, empowerment coach, and mother of five children. I share my story of having a muted voice because of childhood trauma and domestic violence abuse. I am a national and international bestseller who had the honor to be on the billboard two times in Los Angeles and two times in Atlanta. I've had the pleasure of speaking on various platforms and podcasts to empower and inspire others. I am currently pursuing my Master's in Clinical Mental Health Counseling, and I am a member of the American Counseling Association and Alpha Kappa Alpha Sorority, Inc.

YOU ARE ENOUGH

You are Enough to Fulfill the Promises God has Spoken

By Teara F. Stewart

"Not one of all the Lord's good promises to Israel
failed; everyone was FULFILLED."
Joshua 21:45 (NIV)

Have you ever heard the Lord speak to you regarding things He would do in your life? As you go about life, you are looking for the manifestation of those promises but do not see one shred of evidence that it is on the way. In fact, your life reflects quite the opposite. You find yourself having a wilderness experience, one remarkably like the children of Israel.

I know that experience all too well. I have had my fair share of dry places in my life. There were times I just wanted to throw in the towel. I have lost a child, I have been walked out on, I have had those closest to me turn their backs on me. I have felt inadequate. I believed everything negative the enemy said about me. Then, I remembered that I am enough and so are you. You see, those things that the Lord spoke to you regarding the trajectory of your life will all come to pass. There will be some pain; there will be some tests and trials; there will be tears. You may have to cry but hold onto his words. If it is spoken from heaven, it shall not return void.

YOU ARE ENOUGH

I can call back to my remembrance when I was in the fetal position crying until my face was swollen and I had no breath left. I was confused because I knew what I heard, but I did not see anything that reflected those promises. I was in prayer and heard the Lord say clearly, "it will all come to pass in My timing." Now let us be real; that is not what we want to hear, right? We want to hear, "I am getting ready to turn it for you right now." We listen for the messages that say it is coming now, and the storm is over.

When in all actuality, the **weight of the wait** gets even heavier because that is what the Lord does to develop our patience muscles-have us wait. Now the trick is in what we do while we wait. I will tell you it took me a moment to catch on to what I was supposed to be doing besides just praying. I was supposed to be preparing!

That is what I have come to tell you. While you are in the waiting zone, begin to prepare, but if He said it, then you can bank on it happening. Will you be ready when He is ready? Go for all the things that were spoken to you. Hold absolutely nothing back because someone else's next level is tied to you. You are enough! Everything you need you already have. The seeds were placed inside of you while you were being formed in your mother's womb.

You are enough to fulfill the promises God has spoken regarding your life and know that the Lord will make good on everything He said.

BIO:

Teara Stewart is a best-selling author, international speaker, leader, and serial entrepreneur who resides in Louisiana with her husband and three sons. Her mission in life is to create effective change in her community and the lives of those around her.

She is a firm believer that the key to success is believing in yourself. Her faith in God is her guiding light on her journey.

> *"The mindset of the human being is a powerful tool so THINK responsibly."*
>
> Teara

You can reach her via email at:

emerge20@Yahoo.com

Facebook: facebook/teara.stewart.3

Instagram: tearastewart2011

YOU ARE ENOUGH

Wake Up; You Are Unstoppable!
By Dr. Carmen Thomas

"Life takes on new meaning when you become motivated, set goals and charge after them in an unstoppable manner."
Les Brown

In 2006, my real estate biz crashed all around me! I was drowning in a million dollars of debt with less than $30,000 of income, faced with the decision to live or die, give up, or run a new race!

At times, life presents opportunities that are dressed up to look like a failure! You are faced with a decision to ask yourself, "do I have what it takes?" Today, I am here to share with you that "YOU ARE ENOUGH!"

Greatness, goodness, favor, and mercy are at your door for 2021! You are Unstoppable! Tell your "It" to line up or get out of your way because destiny and purpose are assigned to your finish line! Don't miss your opportunity by distractions that get you off track. Press past the pain of procrastination, complacency, rejections, and disappointments! Don't be concerned with fitting in! You are in! You are priceless! You have been bought at the highest price of all! You are Loved! You are Enough! God Loves You and So Do I!!!

Don't miss your destiny and purpose waiting for you at "your" finish line. Keep your eyes 👀 on your prize! God Loves You!

YOU ARE ENOUGH

Be Persistent - Going beyond with or without things, objects, people and learning to push yourself, you are worth the investment. You are your greatest investment.

You are Enough!

Passion and Pain Define Vision - Be precise and concrete, visualizing by faith during the tough times. Invest quality time with you. What keeps you up at night? What problem do you want to solve? Most generally, your vision should be one you've heard before. Be cautious of allowing others to speak to "your" vision that does not agree with you.

Be Present throughout the Process - Being Prepared - Lessons Learned - Being present guides you to discern and listen to understand to make accurate decisions. Identify advisors, coaches, and a team to fulfill the vision early, and when you miss it by placing someone in either role who doesn't fit the framework, remove them quickly.

Transcend when no one is looking - Prayer and meditation early in the morning illuminate your path and provide navigation throughout the journey. You must master what you want to become.

As you discover your best self, practicing and mastering what you would like to become is when you meet and welcome the potential awaiting your arrival.

The process will appear accelerated during the unveiling and discovery of the new you. You must become relentless about staying the course, which makes it easier to eliminate distractions.

Practice Self Talk - Speak positive words of affirmation daily.

Remember your purpose positions you to walk in your Superpower! You Are Enough!!

Your purpose is enormous! It becomes clearer as you take a step of faith in the direction towards your power. Stay in position and continue listening for the voice of the empire you created to evolve and unveil itself!

Whoever Counted You Out Can't Count! Dr. Cheryl Wood

You Are Unstoppable! You are Enough!

BIO:

Dr. Carmen Thomas has been applying transformation to every area of her life since she was a young girl growing up in the projects. She is currently applying servant leadership, transformation, and developing authentic relationships as a professional in her day career as a Chief Government Relations Officer. Dr. Thomas is the Founder of Unstoppable Women's Empire and the Founder of Transformation GEMS, a nonprofit that empowers, educates, and provides resources for women to start and accelerate businesses that create systems, legacies and become recession-proof. Carmen's mission is to empower and inspire women to identify and utilize their gifts to courageously be unstoppable.

YOU ARE ENOUGH

Your Greenhouse of Greatness

By Michelle S. Thomas, *Your Relationship Surgeon*

"When I stand before God at the end of my life, I
would hope that I would not have a single bit of talent
left and could say, I used everything you gave me."
Erma Bombeck

Everyone will experience moments where they become unsure of the outcomes. It is during these moments that greatness is born. Being great is not equivalent to being perfect. There has never been and never will be anyone that can proclaim the status of "perfect." Your greatness is a seed of gifts entrusted to you by God. It is only when you choose to nurture those gifts that your greatness will manifest itself not only to you but to the world!

Now the road to greatness will at times be rocky, lonely, unpaved, and at times may even be "under construction!" The key is to not allow any of those obstacles to deter you from pushing towards your destiny. Be strategic with your moves, be quick to see the obstacles but slow to jump on another path. There are times that your next elevation is right on the other side. If you change paths, U-turn, or even give up too soon, you may be prolonging your win. You must look at each one of those moments as nutrients to build up the endurance of your precious seed. No amount of growth will come without a lot of stretching, pulling, testing, and some setbacks. When you feel that you cannot go on or doubt begins to creep in, you must remember that your gifts are perfectly designed exactly for YOU. The necessary tools to develop your gifts are within your reach. It is during these times that you must protect your undeveloped seed. Avoid comparing your growth to others, don't rush the process, do not cut corners, and never allow anyone to convince you to give up.

Spend time doing a "self-inventory." Find what attributes you naturally encompass to achieve your dreams, and then venture out to obtain the necessary knowledge that you do not have naturally. The most successful entrepreneurs find what they are passionate about and then devise a blueprint on how to capitalize on that. You will not find the greatness set for you by trying to copy someone else's path. Steve Jobs said it best, "Your time is limited, so don't waste it living someone else's life. Don't be trapped by dogma – which is living with the results of other people's thinking. Don't let the noise of other's opinions drown out your own inner voice. And most important, have the courage to follow your heart and intuition. They somehow already know what you truly want to become. Everything else is secondary."

It is not money, status, or family dynamics that will determine your greatness! It is the passion and motivation within you that will get you into places and experiences you have only dreamed possible. True happiness and success are a long-term process, you must always remember to nurture and grow that seed within you continuously, or it will perish. Like every seed, yours comes with its own requirements for its best harvest. You are the caretaker of your "greenhouse" of greatness, now go and produce excellence!

BIO:

Michelle S. Thomas, *Your Relationship Surgeon,* is a two-time Internationally Best-Selling Author, Certified Life/ Relationship/Business Coach, Motivational speaker, and Multiple business owner. She believes that everyone has the power to "touch" their dreams. She has turned her purpose into her profession because she always recognized that real people needed to hear real stories to conquer what really mattered to them. *Your Relationship Surgeon* offers relatable content through her books, coaching, workshops, and motivational speeches designed to elevate your relationship with yourself, your family, and your business.

Website: www.michellesthomas.com

Facebook: https://www.facebook.com/YourRelationshipSurgeon

Instagram: https://www.instagram.com/yourrelationshipsurgeon/

YOU ARE ENOUGH

Grace for The Finish Line
By Simene' Walden

*"God keeps such people so busy enjoying life that they
take no time to brood over the past."*
Ecclesiastes 5:20

What intimidated you will now excite you. Yes, you read that right, and I want you to now scream it loud. WHAT INTIMIDATED ME NOW EXCITES ME!

You see, winning in life and triumphing scared me because I had become accustomed to losing. Victory after victory scared me, so I stopped producing. I would start again and then stop only to realize I was losing momentum and progress. What I thought was hindering me kept me stagnant until I realized the biggest hindrance was what I accepted from others based on the limited knowledge they had and have about me.

Success scared me. Peace scared me. Complete joy scared me. The unconditional love that I did not have to perform to obtain scared me, so anytime I saw a glimpse of what I had never seen before, I would quit. I would either talk myself out of it or allow someone else to talk me out of it because I was afraid. I was dragging fear behind me. Fear was driving me in all kinds of directions, and I was packing it snugly in my suitcase when I traveled. It was not until I got a revelation that the God I serve did not give me the spirit of fear. The God I serve has graciously given me a spirit of power, love, and soundness in my

[281]

mind. Fear is no longer allowed in my space or my head. Fear is of the devil, and since I do not serve him, I now allow grace to carry me for each assignment and task I must perform. God gives grace, and the enemy produces fear.

So, how can I get excited about what used to intimidate me? Allow the grace of God to go before you while goodness and mercy are your entourage. You have to change how you see yourself and what you say about yourself.

We all deal with a level of introspection and extrospection. Introspection or self-reflection is the act or process of looking into oneself. Extrospection is the observance of things outside of oneself. When we look within, we see all of our issues, weaknesses, and flaws, but we also know all of our growth, goals, successes, wins, and strengths.

It is the flaws in us that are usually pointed out that may cause a person to second guess themselves and quit.

Newsflash!!

Your flaws look flawless to someone else. What you hate right now about yourself, someone else is wishing they had.

Everything you thought would disqualify you for your next level of growth and promotion is the very thing that has probably prepared you for it.

Stop worrying about your failures, flaws, and past mistakes, and enjoy the journey to your finish line.

BIO:

Simene' Walden, The Student Teacher, is an Educator, Publisher, Speaker, Book Coach, and Author. She helps educators and leaders tell their stories unapologetically through written and verbal communication. Simene' understands the power of your thought life and heart posture that impacts your speech. Simene' has assisted over 200 women and a few distinguished men within the last few years. If you are looking for a publisher that can help you publish and carry your story, connect with Simene' today. The ABCs of The Student Teacher are A for Academics, B for Books & The Bible, and C for Coaching & Crucial Conversations.

http://www.prettyhealed.com

Email: simene@simenewalden.com

YOU ARE ENOUGH

Let Your Soul Radiate
By Stephanie Wall

"Your worth lies in your soul. You radiate what you have within."
Anoir Ou-Chad

Let your soul radiate; the world NEEDS your GIFTS. I heard it said that the eyes show the strength of the soul as you navigate this life. Enjoy the ride. Treat it like a ride on your favorite roller coaster. Be intentional about being in a state of joy. Throw your hands in the air and scream, "WEEEEEE! There are no do-overs. You have everything that you need to bless the socks off everyone who crosses your path and to reach your goals and dreams. YOU really do. Have fun, be intentional about doing those things that you always wanted to do. When we do the things that we are passionate about, we are working in our purpose, and our very soul radiates.

We are coming out of the worst pandemic of our lifetime. You may have lost one or more family members--- you are still here for a purpose. What is that THING that you always wanted to do? I am talking about that THING that makes your heart SING. What barrier could keep you from getting closer to achieving your goals and dreams? When you are successful...how would you feel? I remember when I finally had the courage, and I wrote my first book. I was so thrilled to see my name on the cover of all the books. My nerves and my joy were operating at the same time. When I saw my name for the first time in print, I cried. My story, being widely known, was mind-blowing at first. Fast-forward to 2021. I had a vision for a book project

[285]

called **"Her Story Our Story - Different Faces, Same Trauma: True Stories of Overcoming."** My sister Pamela, who suffered from severe depression, and had major self-esteem challenges, joined the project. She learned the same lessons that I learned about putting your story on paper. It is super freeing. Don't let anyone else tell your story. Tell it yourself. Don't let the story you have been keeping in your heart and head keep you from growing, loving, leading, or praying. Passionate Motivational Speaker, Les Brown, says *"Many of us are not living our dreams because we are living our fears."*

Today, many of us are still wearing masks to protect ourselves and others. This is a great time to practice smiling with your EYES. Here is the secret…. smile, and your eyes will smile. I dare you to let your soul radiate through your eyes to change the mood, environment, and energy in all the spaces that you are in. If you find yourself listening to the committee in your head, shut it down with a replacement memory or thought of you having done or doing that thing that you always wanted to do. We all have gifts, and only we can provide that gift to the world. Don't miss the opportunity to feel the pride that comes with reaching a goal.

BIO:

Stephanie Wall is a passionate Speaker, Author, and Personal Development Coach who epitomizes the definition of a purpose-driven life; she is committed to advocating for women survivors of trauma. She is a community change agent who served in Law Enforcement for 20 years, with a master's degree in Business and Organizational Leadership. As a certified Coach, she uses empathy and an action-oriented attitude to help people combat life's challenges and inspire Entrepreneurs to set their mindsets for success. Due to her devotion to help women, Stephanie created *Speaker Stephanie LLC*, a personal development brand bridging her passion and career.

YOU ARE ENOUGH

You Are Enough to Carry Your Vision
By Dr. Saundra Wall Williams

*"Enlarge the place of your tent, stretch your tent
curtains wide, do not hold back; lengthen your cords,
strengthen your stakes."*
Isaiah 54:2 (NIV)

On New Year's Day, I watch college football Bowl games with my husband and son. I thought the object of the game was to stop the PLAYER carrying the football from getting into the endzone; however, the object is to keep the FOOTBALL out of the endzone. The opposing team must do everything they can to stop the player from CARRYING the football. This understanding of football will give you a revelation about moving forward with the vision God has for your life and not allowing an opposing team to stop you.

The vision for your life is like the football, and you are the person carrying that vision. You have a God-given vision that you know can help and transform the lives of others. It is a great vision with great purpose, and it cannot be destroyed.

Yet, your opposing team, aka "the enemy," which comes in the form of toxic people, negative relationships, obstacles, struggles, distractions, hindrances, fears, doubt, negative self-talk, and self-limiting beliefs, make you feel as if you are not enough to carry out the plans for the vision God has given you. You feel that "the enemy" is always tackling you.

[289]

YOU ARE ENOUGH

Here's a secret "the enemy" does not want you to know. The "enemy" is not out to destroy *you*. He wants to destroy the *vision* you are carrying. Why? There are two reasons: 1) The vision for your life has a purpose, and 2) Executing that vision will stretch and strengthen your faith!

God has given you great vision to serve others. Yet, there are times when you are overwhelmed with life, family, relationships, work, or ministry. How will the vision come to fruition through you if you have limitations and challenges?

When God gives you a vision to carry out, He empowers you to accomplish it. Plus, His plan comes with every resource that you will need to accomplish it (1 Thessalonians 5:24).

God has chosen YOU to execute the vision He has given you. He built you specifically for that purpose. You are enough to carry out the plan and vision God has for you. God designed this vision before you were born (Jeremiah 1:5). The struggles you experience are components of God's unique plan for you. The opposition you face is an attempt to keep you from the success God has already planned for you. Your vision may have pain and disappointments. Don't hold on to the pain; reach for the possibility!

With possibility comes expansion. Expansion will require you to go outside of your comfort zone. The vision you are carrying requires you to be comfortable with being uncomfortable. Carrying the vision in the midst of discomfort is critical to your success.

The vision God has placed in your heart is valuable. You must carry it out regardless of how many times your opposing team knocks you down. Regardless of your current challenges, know that carrying your vision to its end zone is what God built you to do.

[290]

BIO:

Dr. Saundra Wall Williams equips emerging and established women leaders to increase their influence, impact, and income by building themselves and executing their vision. She founded the Vision Building Institute, a premier online training and leadership development company that focuses on coaching, mentorship, motivation, and accountability. Dr. Saundra, also an ordained minister, retired as the Sr. Vice President of the North Carolina Community College System and turned her passion for women in leadership into a prosperous enterprise. She has delivered hundreds of workshops, coaching sessions, keynotes, seminars, and training programs. She serves on corporate boards and boards in higher education.

YOU ARE ENOUGH

You Are Enough to S.L.A.Y. Your Finances

By Dr. Ranelli A. Williams, CPA

"Slay your finances, or your finances will slay you."
Dr. Ranelli A. Williams, CPA

A first-year college student who never really discussed money with her family finds herself applying for credit cards on the college campus and ends up accumulating debt for most of her young adult life. Before she realized what was happening, she was thousands of dollars in debt and had already developed such poor spending habits that she repeated the cycle over and over again.

That first-year college student was me. I had such a destructive relationship with money that it almost cost my family our home and our business. What I can tell you is that being financially slain is not a unique circumstance. Many people find themselves in an array of money issues and clueless about how to dig themselves out of the tangled financial web they are wrapped in. Stressed and feeling totally beaten down, they begin accepting the lie that they do not have what it takes to move beyond where they are because they spend their time focused on the mountain of financial issues they face. As a result, they remain in a vicious cycle of living paycheck to paycheck, robbing Peter to pay Paul, riddled in debt, leaving a legacy of bills to their children, running a business year after year with no predictable income, and the list goes on. Can you identify? As I have found and can attest, the good news is there is hope for positive change. Here are

[293]

four ways to S.L.A.Y. your finances so that your finances do not slay you.

Way #1: Seek to reconcile your relationship with money. Your relationship with money affects your spending habits and earning power. Start the reconciliation process by recognizing that money is a tool to help you reach your goals; acknowledging your responsibility of being a good financial steward; and realizing that wanting wealth does not make you bad or greedy.

Way #2: Look at money as a tool to help you reach your goals. When you allow yourself to dream beyond bills and focus on the things that matter to you most, you experience financial peace. You position yourself to create a clear vision of how you can become a good financial steward and use money as the tool it is to achieve your most important goals and dreams in life.

Way #3: Acknowledge your responsibility of being a good financial steward. A steward is responsible for wisely managing that which was entrusted to him or her. Likewise, you should effectively manage the financial resources you receive, and the reward is reduced financial stress and building wealth.

Way #4: Yield not to false ideas that wanting wealth makes you bad and greedy. Building wealth is not bad or greedy. Rather, it is a means of empowering you to take care of your current and future needs, giving back to others, and leaving an inheritance to your children's children. With this awareness, my charge to you is go, "relentlessly activate wealth" unapologetically, S.L.A.Y.

BIO:

Dr. Ranelli A. Williams is a CPA, financial educator, profit strategist, bestselling author, and award-nominated speaker.

She is a Co-Founder with her husband, Eric of ERJ Services, where they provide profit-focused and strategic consulting services so that service-based entrepreneurs are equipped to make sense of their numbers and empowered to build strong financial legacies that lead to generational wealth.

Dr. Ranelli also founded R.A.W. Legacy Solutions to provide mindset and money solutions to help female career professionals thrive financially, so they can not only start and run the cash-rich and profitable businesses they care about but also build a debt-free legacy.

Connect with Dr. Ranelli @drranelliwilliams on Facebook, IG, and LinkedIn or emailing support@ranelliwilliams.com.

YOU ARE ENOUGH

Own Your Power: It's Your Fearless Force Within

By Carolyn Wilson

"You can be pitiful, or you can be powerful, but you can't be both."
Joyce Meyer.

Have you ever found yourself in a situation that you didn't quite know how you got there? Have you ever been through something so devastating that it leaves you questioning why you had to experience it? Or have you ever felt like no matter how hard you tried, nothing ever seemed right? Like there is this force keeping you from reaching anything meaningful personally, professionally, financially, even spiritually. It feels like something major is missing from your life that you cannot quite put your finger on. If you resonate with any of this, then just know you are not alone as this was once me.

Today's Carolyn understands the essence of healing by releasing her own limiting beliefs. This mindset shift cultivated her personal weight loss, mindfulness, positive thinking, and overcoming trauma & abuse experiences. For Starters, becoming a featured expert on Dr. Oz and Women's World Magazine surely isn't the same Carolyn of yesteryears.

The Carolyn from before was one that felt pitiful, unloved, different, embarrassed, alone, isolated, depleted, depressed, unworthy, invisible, and broken. I spent many years carrying guilt and shame of being molested by my biological father, including the life that followed riddled with abusive relationships, teenage pregnancy, single parenthood, family court, welfare, evictions, and expulsions leading to one failure after another.

After several decades, I reluctantly accepted that this was my life even though I felt deep down like there was something more. Unfortunately, I ignored that constant nagging feeling by showing up in the world like I wasn't enough despite what I felt. So, the world treated me exactly how I told it to. Unbeknownst to me, I was conditioning myself to avoid what was for me while gravitating towards what was not— merely operating on autopilot towards a perpetual life of dysfunction.

Have you ever felt like you were on autopilot? Have you ever said "I'm Fine" when you weren't because you didn't want to deal with your truth? Have you ever ignored that pesky feeling trying to convince you there was more?

If so, then let me tell you there is more! You can regain control of this force that has been inactivated all your life. That provoking feeling is called your Power! And it wants to be activated! It's something innately within you making you a force to be reckoned with that's Powerful! Once I decided to no longer ignore the nudge of my own power, I changed. And so, can you!

Giving my power permission to exist allowed me to face my burdens. Just know you'll have to get down and dirty with it even when it hurts. Trust me when I say the relief you get once the pain of ignoring your power (not your burdens) goes away undoubtedly; it's life-altering. I'm here to be a testament that once you embrace and own your power, you become the pilot realizing and believing that you are enough. Thus, the world will treat you as the Powerful Force that you are!!

BIO:

Carolyn Wilson of Magnify Your Essence is The Fearless Magnified Educator™. An award-winning filmmaker, bestselling author, international speaker, and health & wellness expert featured on ABC, CBS, Dr. Oz, IheartRadio, Radio One, Huffington Post, and Woman's World Magazine. A Sexual Child Abuse and Domestic Violence Survivor turned advocate who intentionally created a transformative healing journey establishing her new life's narrative. Her soul mission is to educate women globally on overcoming fear, manifesting their best life fearlessly (especially after trauma & abuse), aligning mind, body, & spirit to heal for their divine purpose—visit: bit.ly/manifestbestlife to manifest your best life.

YOU ARE ENOUGH

You Are Right!

By Darius "The Professor" Wise

"The Greatest Journey is the Journey of the mind.
This determines the Journey of life."
Darius Wise

What you believe is not necessarily grounded in fact. The foundation of what we believe is driven by the thoughts that we consistently have over time. Our thoughts create emotions. Once an emotion is attached to a thought, then a belief is developed. Based on that belief, we create behaviors that determine the actions we take in life.

As we think, our thoughts program our unconscious mind. The power of this process is that you cannot be wrong to yourself. Whatever you think and believe, you are right! The human brain is not capable, on its own, of determining fact from fiction. So, if you think you are not enough, you are right. If you think you cannot be successful, you are right. But also, if you think you can accomplish your wildest dreams, you are right.

Over 20 years ago, I had the idea that I should write a book. But, unconsciously, I didn't believe that I had the ability to write a book and become an author. This belief manifested itself in my life by me attempting to write a book and never getting past a few uninspiring paragraphs. I vividly remember the conversations that I would have with myself and how discouraging they were. As I look back over that time, I can see how I talked myself out of the idea that I could write a book and created the belief that I would never become an author.

James Allen, the author of the book *As A Man Thinketh,* said, "As a man thinketh in his heart, so is he. A man is literally what he thinks. His character being the complete sum of all his thoughts." Simply put, your world without will be a reflection of your world within. Once I read this, I was inspired, and you should be too. This lets you know that it is by your own thinking that you can build the weapons to destroy yourself or you can create the tools to build yourself up.

If the circumstances of your life are not what you desire, you have the power within to change your outcomes by changing how and what you think. This begins with changing the conversations you have with yourself. The internal conversations you have are the most powerful and important conversations you will ever have. The thoughts you have must be positive, clear, unchangeable and consistent.

By changing my thoughts, and in-turn changing what I believed, I was able to write a book. You have the ability to accomplish what you desire by being aware of your thoughts. And if they don't align with your desires, change what you are thinking. This process doesn't happen overnight, but if you are consistent and persistent, you can reprogram your unconscious mind and become the phenomenal person you were created to be.

To believe you are enough, you first have to think the thought that you are enough!

BIO:

Darius inspires, encourages, and helps people understand the connection between their mindset, skillset, and environment. Aptly nicknamed, The Professor, Darius is committed to helping people take control of their Phenomenal mind and consciously use it every day to achieve their goals. An author, speaker, and neuro-life coach, he delivers revolutionary truths, adaptable tools, and key actions to a wide range of audiences on all media platforms – television, radio, and social media. Success principles, neuroscience, humor, and real-life experiences are organically infused into every presentation. Darius is the founder and CEO of WiseDecisions, LLC.

YOU ARE ENOUGH

Winning in Life at Your Pace
By Dr. Debra Wright Owens

"Slow and Steady Wins the Race."
Robert Lloyd

You don't have to cross life's finish line first to win the race. But you must give all that you have to your race. Life is more about running your race at your pace and less about who crosses the finish line first. Truthfully, I do not suspect that many are eager to cross life's finish line first and would much rather prolong life's journey for as long as possible.

The adversities and obstacles encountered along life's journey can seem overwhelming at times. They can even cause us to question whether we can continue or go any further. Many throw in the towel along the way and call it quits, unaware that they were on the verge of a breakthrough that would have given them the second wind they needed to continue. Nevertheless, they could not see beyond where they were at the time or lost all hope and convinced themselves that they just didn't have the fuel to go on. If only they had realized that they already possessed the answers deep within. If only they had known that they were ENOUGH! You are enough. We are enough. Enough to be exactly who we are meant to be and enough to do exactly what we have been put on earth to do!

Remember, *"the race is not to the swift..."* Ecclesiastes 9:11 – but to those who "stay the course." You don't have to run another's race, only yours. Focus on your vision, your purpose, and your goals. Focus on maximizing your potential and impacting the world. Focus on being the best you. Focus on building a legacy for generations that will come after you. When we try to keep up with others, we lose focus on our own race, identity, and abilities. Comparison kills confidence and causes us to become discouraged and some to ultimately quit.

Commit to your own life's race. If you find yourself feeling overwhelmed and gasping for breath, it may be that your pace is too fast, and you need to slow down. Going too fast can sometimes cause us to stumble. So, it is perfectly okay to slow down if you need to – to refuel and reset! Taking on a slower pace will allow you to regain control, refocus on your goals and what's ahead of you, as well as revive you for continuing the race towards your life's goals, dreams, and desires. Pace yourself for maximum productivity. Don't burn out along the way and forfeit the victory. Pace yourself with the end goal in mind. Stay focused, fit, and faithful – and don't you dare quit! You are more than enough to accomplish every dream and desire that is burning deep within your core, waiting to be birthed. I challenge you to accept that you are enough!

BIO:

Dr. Debra Wright Owens, a native Mississippian, is an empowerment advocate, certified professional coach, author, speaker, and minister. She is the Founder/CEO of Encore Empowerment International, LLC, a professional service firm specializing in top-tier business and professional development solutions. She is the Founder/CEO of The Visionaire Foundation, Inc, a global movement dedicated to enhancing others' lives through education, knowledge, and selfless service. She is a full-time practicing HR professional with over 33 years of federal service, earning a Ph.D. in Business Management, an MPA, and BAS. She has two amazing children, whom she truly adores.

Made in the USA
Middletown, DE
24 June 2021

43099482R00170